White pigeons surround visitors at the great mosque of Mazar-e-Sharif, in Afghanistan—
a shrine so holy that legend says gray birds turn white here within forty days.

VICTOR ENGLEBERT

Rainbow-crowned, Fatu Hiva in the Marquesas rises from the Pacific.

Prepared by the Special Publications Division
National Geographic Society, Washington, D. C.

Secret

Corners of the World

SECRET CORNERS OF THE WORLD

Contributing Authors: LESLIE ALLEN,
JAMES BILLIPP, TOR EIGELAND, VICTOR ENGLEBERT,
NOEL GROVE, JANE R. MCCAULEY

Contributing Photographers: SAM ABELL,
JAMES BILLIPP, TOR EIGELAND, VICTOR ENGLEBERT,
ROLAND and SABRINA MICHAUD, JAMES A. SUGAR

Published by THE NATIONAL GEOGRAPHIC SOCIETY
GILBERT M. GROSVENOR, *President*
MELVIN M. PAYNE, *Chairman of the Board*
OWEN R. ANDERSON, *Executive Vice President*
ROBERT L. BREEDEN, *Vice President, Publications
and Educational Media*

Prepared by THE SPECIAL PUBLICATIONS DIVISION
DONALD J. CRUMP, *Editor*
PHILIP B. SILCOTT, *Associate Editor*
WILLIAM L. ALLEN, WILLIAM R. GRAY, *Senior Editors*

Staff for this book
MARY ANN HARRELL, *Managing Editor*
JANE R. MCCAULEY, *Project Editor*
CHARLES E. HERRON, *Picture Editor*
JOSEPHINE B. BOLT, *Art Director*
PENNY DIAMANTI DE WIDT, PATRICIA F. FRAKES,
CATHERINE HERBERT HOWELL,
ALICE K. JABLONSKY, *Researchers*

Illustrations and Design
CYNTHIA B. SCUDDER, *Assistant Designer*
JANET DYER, D. RANDY YOUNG, *Design Assistants*
JOHN D. GARST, JR., PATRICIA K. CANTLAY,
JUDITH BELL SIEGEL, *Map Research, Design,
and Production*
LESLIE ALLEN, WILLIAM P. BEAMAN, TONI EUGENE,
CHRISTINE ECKSTROM LEE, JANE R. MCCAULEY,
JENNIFER C. URQUHART, *Picture Legend Writers*

Engraving, Printing, and Product Manufacture
ROBERT W. MESSER, *Manager*
GEORGE V. WHITE, *Production Manager*
GREGORY STORER, *Production Project Manager*
MARK R. DUNLEVY, RICHARD A. MCCLURE,
RAJA D. MURSHED, DAVID V. SHOWERS,
   Assistant Production Managers
KATHERINE H. DONOHUE, *Senior Production Assistant*
KATHERINE R. LEITCH, *Production Staff Assistant*

NANCY F. BERRY, PAMELA A. BLACK, NETTIE BURKE,
JANE H. BUXTON, MARY ELIZABETH DAVIS,
CLAIRE M. DOIG, ROSAMUND GARNER,
VICTORIA D. GARRETT, MARY JANE GORE,
JANE R. HALPIN, NANCY J. HARVEY, SHERYL A. HOEY,
JOAN HURST, ARTEMIS S. LAMPATHAKIS,
VIRGINIA A. MCCOY, MERRICK P. MURDOCK,
CLEO PETROFF, VICTORIA I. PISCOPO,
TAMMY PRESLEY, CAROL A. ROCHELEAU,
KATHERYN M. SLOCUM, JENNY TAKACS, *Staff Assistants*

MARY KATHLEEN HOGAN, *Index*

HARDCOVER: *A compass rose evokes the age of exploration, the lure of novel
destinations on the byways of the earth.*

Autumn—in April—brings color to southern beeches

in Argentine Tierra del Fuego. Flooding caused by beavers killed the denuded trees.

5

Introduction

For many of us, the first glimpse of faraway places came in the pages of NATIONAL GEOGRAPHIC; and this book continues the Society's tradition of portraying lands and peoples off the beaten tracks of the world.

In one instance, it records a land on the eve of calamity: northern Afghanistan, for centuries a crossroads of trade and thus of civilization, now closed to travelers while Soviet forces confront a bitter resistance. This chapter blends photographs from recent, peaceful years, and a vivid text prepared with the help of Afghan advisers. One of these, scholar and statesman Mohammad Siddiq Farhang, suggests the remoteness of his homeland in the 1920s: "My first glimpse of the West? I was just a boy, living in a village, and my father brought home some books: Jules Verne's novels—*Around the World in Eighty Days,* and *Twenty Thousand Leagues Under the Sea*—had been translated from French to Turkish to Farsi. Those stories showed me that there would be a different world to study."

To bridge comparable distances—but in a lighter mood—this book introduces the little-known communities of the Alpujarras, in southern Spain, left in obscurity for some three centuries after the Christian forces from the north defeated its Moorish rulers. It also presents the enigmatic snow-clad Santa Marta range that overlooks the Caribbean Sea, and Indians who took refuge there from the Spanish conquerors who founded present-day Colombia.

One chapter captures the quirks of travel in the Marquesas, isles off the sea lanes and jet routes of the contemporary Pacific. "Coming here," says one of the residents of Nuku Hiva, "is an adventure—not a vacation." Another account reveals the eerie wilds of Africa's equatorial mountains, the Ruwenzori, the Virunga volcanoes, the game-rich plains between and the hospitable people who help get trucks out of the mire and strangers out of confusion. And another ranges south to the uncluttered vistas of Tierra del Fuego and Cape Horn, where the poignance of the phrase "land's end" gains force in a setting of bleakness—and beauty.

In this lattermost region the Society carries on the task it assumed in 1890, of fostering research and exploration. Since 1970 its grants have supported Natalie Goodall's studies, first of the flora of Tierra del Fuego and now of the smaller sea mammals abundant in its waters. Today few ships risk the notorious tempests of Cape Horn; but nature's challenges to science are greater now than ever, there and worldwide, and the Society's members help to meet them.

Therefore we hope that they will find pride as well as pleasure in these accounts of far and varied destinations: places unfamiliar to many, yet dear to some with the special charm of home. — MARY ANN HARRELL
Managing Editor

Deep in Zaire's Ituri Forest—one of Africa's grandest—waters of the Isehe River cascade over ledges of Mont Hoyo. "It's near the Equator, but it's cool, up in a tumultuous landscape of hills. Here you're a long way from civilization," says far-traveled photographer Jim Sugar; "it's the most remote place I've ever seen."

In the Alpujarras country of southern Spain, milch cows often double as draft animals; this man of

Pampaneira plows a patch of land before sowing lentils.

9

The Marquesas

By Victor Englebert
Photographs by the Author

A setting full moon, flooding the ocean with silvery light, is outlining to the west a scene of nightmare: the island of Tahuata, a gigantic black fortress brooding over the waves. To the east her pallid brightness robs Mohotani of all mystery. Hiva Oa, which we left two hours earlier, sinks behind us; and moonset will come before we reach Fatu Hiva, most southerly of the Marquesas group. Already the east grows pale. On Tahuata the blacks and whites turn gray, and the phantoms vanish.

Our small fishing boat is leaping nimbly over the hard-pounding swell. My fellow passengers—four women from Fatu Hiva and a French official on a tour of duty—sit in sleepy silence.

The sun rises, and with it rise wind and waves. Who ever called this ocean Pacific? Three of the passengers are leaning overboard. A crewman sloshes bucketfuls of seawater on the deck to clean it, carelessly soaking my feet. "Are you a sailor?" he asks. "You hold well your stomach!"

I shrug off the compliment, for I am a landlubber who has taken a sea-sickness pill. A Belgian who has wandered over three continents and who has come to the Marquesas to sample a different wilderness. Having lived in Colombia for eight years, I have often stood on the South American shore of the Pacific and felt the pull of its horizon.

A Spanish mariner, Alvaro de Mendaña de Neira, felt that restlessness four centuries ago. Sailing from Peru in 1595, he discovered Fatu Hiva and the three other southern islands of the group. Two hundred years would pass before the rest were discovered—by the Englishman James Cook, the American Joseph Ingraham, the Frenchman Etienne Marchand. Of the ten notable islands, four—including Mohotani—are uninhabited today.

Four wave-tossed hours bring us to the tormented volcanic relief of Fatu Hiva. In its lee we enter quiet water, yet have a precarious landing at Omoa, the main village. As we anchor, a sleek outrigger races toward us, one man steering, two paddling. They take us ashore on the rush of a large wave—and we almost founder. Luckily, my photographic equipment is in watertight plastic bags. Yelling and bailing and pulling wildly on the paddles, our Marquesans get us back on course. In the shallows we all jump out to drag the canoe up the strand for unloading.

Unlike other isles of Polynesia, the Marquesas are not protected by coral reefs, and approaching them is often a delicate enterprise. Their isolation, rugged terrain, and lack of development increase the surprises they set in the way of seasoned travelers. I learn this at once.

Some spectators have quietly watched our arrival. One refers me, for

Paradise found: Volcanic spires soar above Ua Pu, in the South Pacific's Marquesas Islands. Village boat shelters fringe the shore, a reminder of Polynesian traditions surviving in an island group little touched by the 20th-century world.

accommodation, to the local shopkeeper and lends me a wheelbarrow to transport my baggage. Nobody cares to help me, even for money. So I trundle my luggage up the village's main alley, between two rows of lush gardens exploding with the colors of hibiscus and bougainvillea, past brightly painted plywood bungalows. I find my man in his well-stocked shop, and follow the girl whom he has told to show me a house.

"Here it is," she says, leading me into a rather grubby bungalow. "I will clean it for you." She says "*pour toi*," not "*pour vous*," for Marquesans do not bother with the formalities of French. And picking a broom from a dusty corner, she sweeps the floor, the curtains, the table, and the bed.

Two Frenchmen live in Omoa, and I meet them that day. They are, each in his own way, typical of white men who settle in the South Seas.

Lionel, in his early thirties, married a Fatu Hivan while serving in the French navy and has retired here to a rented house. Full of energy and dreams, he plans to build a house and cultivate land that his wife owns in a distant valley. "I work alone," he says. "I have so much time on my hands that I need no help. I want to buy a secondhand bulldozer to open a road to my wife's land. Then I will plant fruit trees and travel to Australia, the United States, and Japan to market my crop."

Yet the Fatu Hivans have more land than they can use, and live comfortably with little effort. How does Lionel hope to get his fruit picked one day? Have these islands not deceived him, as they deceive others?

Philippe, 27, sailed alone from France on a six-meter yacht two years ago. Now he is trying his hand at agriculture. But having no Marquesan wife, he has no land, and without money he cannot buy any. Indeed, much

In the path of southeast trade winds and rolling seas that sweep 4,000 miles from South America, the rugged Marquesas spangle the Pacific. Wind and wave brought settlers to the group two thousand years ago; two centuries after their European discovery in 1595, adventurers, colonizers, missionaries, and romantics stepped ashore. Annexed by France in 1842, the isles form an administrative division of French Polynesia today.

land is held jointly by members of very large families, and strangers with money may not find suitable land for sale. Mostly he works as a copra sharecropper—gathering coconuts, cutting them up for drying. One morning I follow him as he goes out to harvest wild coffee.

Leaving at seven, we climb for an hour over risky terrain, along a steep and muddy path overlooking a sheer drop, up a network of banyan roots clutching a 25-foot cliff, finally up a 20-foot rope. Then Philippe hacks his way to the wild trees to pick the scanty berries. He earns the equivalent of $15 for a 12-hour day. He makes much less on his other crops. Perhaps, as rumor says, it is unrequited love that keeps him here.

I rent an outrigger and sail along the cliff-bound coast to see the spectacular bay of Hanavave, also called Bay of the Virgins, where pinnacles of basalt guard the entrance to a high-walled valley. Shyly, women of Hanavave show me how they pound bark to make tapa cloth; and a young man agrees to put me on the way to Omoa, for I want to walk back across the highlands, remnants of two concentric volcanic craters.

He leads me to the foot of the inner cone and shows me the path. "You cannot get lost," he says. "Only remember, when you come to a fork, to take the path to the right. You should reach Omoa in a few hours."

I thank him and walk up—through *mape* forest, then over low ferns— the mountain trail which offers breathtaking views over the island and the sea. At the base of a deep canyon the houses of Hanavave shrink to the size of dice. The landscape is at once beautiful and somber, charged with foreboding. Like the other islands of the archipelago, Fatu Hiva once had a larger and happier population. Famines, intertribal wars, and above all the diseases brought by the white man wiped out 90 percent of it. And the dark valleys seem burdened with terrible memories.

I lose the sense of time and distance. When I reach a fork, I veer right and down through prickly shrubs. Across the valley, white goats balance on a narrow ledge to browse. Like other "wild" animals of the Marquesas— cattle, horses, sheep, goats, and cats—they descend from domestic stock introduced by Europeans. Below me, horses are grazing. At length I realize that I am following a path they opened, not a traveler's route.

I climb the mountain again. Another fork takes me on a new leg-chafing expedition to nowhere. Back on the ridge, a white veil of rain sweeps over me, torrential and cold. The path becomes slippery as I skirt abysses, then so overgrown as to be almost impassable. It turns into a narrow gutter, wide enough for one foot. To my right rises the mountain wall; bushes force me away from it. I stumble and fall against the shrubbery.

No, into a void! I see nothing under me except the crown of a tree. My heart jerks as I scramble for a handhold. I check my fall, and, with camera bag heavy on my arm and sweat cold on my skin, I pull myself back onto the trail.

Shaken, I return to open heights to orient myself. At last, through the pouring rain, I can descry my path far ahead. The light is dimming, but the landscape is so beautiful that I cannot make myself hurry. Suddenly, seven white cows appear on a hill. They charge toward me ribs against ribs, agile as fighting bulls. Luckily, they veer away. They are domestic stock— that is, they have owners—but they are dangerous. To kill them for the table is the work of a hunter. The great hunt for "barnyard" animals strikes me as characteristic of the Marquesas in its oddity.

Dusk finds me walking down a gallery of mango trees, whose fruits relieve my thirst, to a dirt road. This is being built to allow three jeeps in Omoa to visit Hanavave some day. Cheerfully, I lengthen my steps. But the road is a river of mud. I travel much of it on the seat of my pants.

When I reach Omoa, the fervent and lovely voices of the villagers are ringing from the little church. How I wish I could hear traditional music also, chants from centuries past, before the missionaries broke the Marquesans' idols and prohibited their dances. Surely the people were less reserved and suspicious then—did not lend gloom to their mountains.

Travel between islands can be as chancy as travel across one. The administrative boat arrives, and I get permission to embark on it for Hiva Oa. Two men in a dinghy come for me, but the waves are so violent that they cannot use the beach: I wait on a rocky shore above deep water. They paddle in, ready to paddle back before the surf smashes them. In the moment between waves I throw them my luggage. They come back for me.

"Jump!" they shout. But how do you jump into a canoe that presents its prow for a fraction of a second, too far below and too far away from a rock pounded by furious breakers? Ashamed, I watch them withdraw.

"Jump!" they call more earnestly when they return.

And I jump—right over the head of the first man. They take me out to the boat, which plunges headlong into a heavy sea. Night has come, and rain is falling.

Classic island beauty shines from the face of Florence Kaimuko, of Hiva Oa. When Captain James Cook explored the Marquesas in 1774, he called their people "the finest race . . . in this Sea." In 1838 French missionaries began to introduce the now-dominant Roman Catholic faith; their successors brought such secular pastimes as bingo. Women in the Hiva Oa village of Atuona play this game with shells or stones or other makeshift markers (opposite).

At 1 a.m., when I reach Atuona, nobody is around. I camp under the porch of the town hall. At 6 sharp, doors open and a sudden flow of people sweeps up the road on foot, on motorcycles, and in cars. Curious, I entrust my luggage to public honesty—theft is rare in the Marquesas—and follow them.

Saying hello left and right, receiving cool greetings in return, I reach the goal of this early bustle: a fast-shrinking mountain of crisp, fragrant French bread at a Chinese bakery. The villagers snatch the loaves up by the armful. Marquesan families are large enough to eat 12 or 15 of these *baguettes* every day.

While waiting for accommodation, I climb to the small cemetery above the bay. Since the great French painter Paul Gauguin was buried here, it has become a place of pilgrimage, and now Jacques Brel, the famous Belgian singer and composer, is buried near him. They wanted to die in peace, and they could not have found a better place than the Marquesas. Here they were as far from the world as one could ever be, and with as discreet a people as they could ever find.

Back in the village I pass a group of children agitating a makeshift flag and singing *"Allons enfants de la Patrie, Le jour de gloire est arrivé."* Rehearsing for the national day? July 14 will be on us soon.

At the town hall I am given the key to a clean little bungalow, and after a shower I return to wait for the mayor, Guy Rauzy, one of the Marquesas' two delegates to the Territorial Assembly in Tahiti. He is admired for efficiency and foresight as well as for influence over the French administrators. In Atuona the young welcome his development projects. Yet some say he does not share his power enough; and in other islands people complain that he does too much for Hiva Oa and not enough for them.

Rauzy arrives around eight, a middle-aged man with a flower-trimmed straw hat, three-quarters French by descent and four-quarters so in feature. Also a good Marquesan, born and brought up here, fluent in the language. He gives me information in abundance, and presents me to Aroma Raihauti, his aide *extraordinaire*. He lends me Aroma's help, and a jeep, for the length of my stay on Hiva Oa.

An intelligent young athlete, Aroma stands nearly six feet tall, with the face of a desert Arab, the hair of a black-maned lion, and the largest feet I have ever seen. He is the most talkative Marquesan I will ever meet, and while he drives me about he tells me of recent events. When the Marquesas were dependent on administrators in Tahiti, he says, they were neglected. Since 1972 they have had elections, for national office as well as local. "And now that our voice is being heard we have been equipped with roads and electricity!"

Passing the bay, where seven or eight yachts swing at anchor, he points out a breakwater under construction. "Soon we shall have quiet mooring there!" He tells me plans for a tuna fishery and other projects.

What excites him most is television, introduced in 1979, one public set per village. Aroma schedules the programs—a cassette every night from 7 to 9, with an extra hour of international news on Saturday. "TV has become immensely popular," he says. "Besides relieving us from boredom, it helps people keep up their French. And it keeps us in contact with the world—remember, we have no newspapers here, and our four new bungalows are enough for visitors at Atuona. Fatu Hiva and Tahuata do not have TV yet, but how they press for it!"

Next day Aroma drives me to Puamau, a village on the other side of the island, for a sense of the ancient past. We climb steadily through a varied vegetation dominated by mango, pandanus, and the ironwood or *toa* trees once used for the carving of war clubs. We pass open land carpeted with low ferns. Green buttresses radiate from the island's razor-sharp crest to the sea all around, and remnants of forest shelter in their deep folds. Our winding road affords vistas of the coast, while the sun outlines ridges with rays of light or floods them with gold, and fills bays with crinkling silver or azure.

We cross a natural bridge, where steep slopes fall away on each side. We descend in hairpins so sharp that Aroma has to maneuver back and forth above a precipice at each bend. We pass valleys brimming with coconut trees, tiny villages of two or three houses. Puamau is well worth the disconcerting moments—a fine white-sand beach rims its spectacular bay.

Driving up its smiling valley between gardens beckoning with color, bird songs, and clear rivulets, we go to see the *tikis,* stone idols famous in the Marquesas. They are large, eight to eleven feet tall, but to me hardly impressive. One has lost its head, possibly at the hands of missionaries; another, identified as a pregnant woman, reminds me of a frog; a third stands eroded past recognition. All are weatherworn, and mosquitoes defend them fiercely. So we return to enjoy the beach.

In late afternoon we begin our three-hour ride back. Aroma pulls a gun from under a blanket. "This is the hour when wild chickens come out of the bush," he says. And he kills three in half an hour. We pick papayas from roadside trees. "Is life not wonderfully easy here?" remarks Aroma.

Catches of the day, Marquesan style, reflect a blend of European and Polynesian cultures. French bread and imported snacks fill the arms of a youngster on Ua Pu (opposite) after a trip to the bakery. On Ua Huka, a girl holds a fresh yellow-finned tuna, perhaps to be marinated and served raw as ika tee, *a traditional delicacy.*

Yet strangers may not profit so freely from nature's generosity, as young Philippe has learned on Fatu Hiva. Although some Marquesans would welcome tourism, none wants an influx of foreign settlers. With a total population of nearly 6,000, the Marquesans could too easily become a minority in their own islands.

The sun sets over the sea in a changing display of warm colors. As we approach Atuona we pass two men on horseback, with big bloodstained sacks. Dogs lope along with them. Aroma exchanges a few words with them, then tells me they are hunters who have killed a wild cow. The dogs would track an animal that escaped wounded.

No such excitement marks the days in Atuona. One afternoon I stop at the single restaurant for a Coke, wondering where all the people have gone. Some sit in a government office, some work on a construction site, but the others? I hear voices behind a low wall—many voices. I investigate: 21 women are sitting on the floor playing bingo for money, with shells for markers. This, I learn, they do every day.

Slowly I make acquaintances, and one night a banquet brings about fifty people to the restaurant. They drink red wine, and they seem eager to talk to me. I am surprised, and admit it.

"Oh," says one, "we sit back watching newcomers for a long time before accepting them."

"How do you like it here?" asks another. "I always liked Hiva Oa—but since I did my military service in France and saw Paris, I love Hiva Oa! How can anybody live in Paris?"

"Why is it," asks someone else, "that you Europeans almost always come here without your wives? Are they afraid of cannibals?"

Now the group speaks freely on this notorious topic. Do they want to make light of it, or to provoke me? One young man reminds me that the Marquesan population in Captain Cook's day has been estimated at 100,000, and says, "No wonder they were eating each other!"

One sunny morning, I hear that *Taporo II* has arrived. She is a schooner subsidized by the French government to serve the islands, and is bringing schoolchildren home for vacation—those of grade four and up must study in Atuona or on Nuku Hiva, in Taiohae. She can take me over to Tahuata. I pack quickly, and reluctantly say good-bye to my friend Aroma.

While the boat lies at anchor, the children scamper up and down and around and pilfer food from the galley. The young cook pretends not to see. But when we enter the agitated waters of the Bordelais Channel, the youngsters fall silent; they lie down or sit or clutch the rail in pathetic misery. They revive when we reach calmer water to leeward of Tahuata, and watch the coast go by till we enter the beautiful bay of Vaitahu.

Here all the children of Tahuata go ashore by dinghy. But the mayor escorts some of them back. It is too dangerous, he says, for speedboats to take children to Hana Tetena, on the windward coast. He demands that the schooner do it, and the captain agrees.

"Poor kids," says the mayor as he shoulders one of my duffel bags and leads me to the home of a family that will rent a room. "You should see the landing at Hana Tetena! The sea there is so violent that boats cannot get near the coast. You have to swim ashore, and if you cannot, they pull you in with a rope."

My new friend Tehaumate Tetahiotupa is not only mayor but also a schoolmaster. He has a little daughter who has just returned from a convent school in Atuona, and he worries about education in the Marquesas. "My daughter is safe with the nuns," he says. "She will complete her studies. But boys have to board with the villagers, who do not feel entitled to discipline the children of others. So our boys come back swearing, drinking, smoking, and listening to cassettes—that is, to strange foreign music—and may drop out after the fourth or fifth grade."

Two teenage boys, Tana and Tea, join me next day on a long walk over the crest of the island and down the other side to Moto Pu. Along the way they point out oddities and identify trees like *burau,* used for canoes, and ironwood. Papaya trees line the road, grown from seed spread by birds.

"Pour les cochons," says Tea. For the pigs—too many for human consumption. We pick a ripe one and share it on the spot.

Tea speaks dreadful French, but is more talkative than the sophisticated Tana. I strain to understand him, pretend to when I cannot. Our hike yields brilliant moments: Vaitahu far below, dazzling as a movie creation; lovely and uninhabited bays with white beaches and strange names. Once, suddenly, we hear a resounding *cocorico* from a wild rooster. Tana has brought an air gun; it misfires, and the bird escapes.

Tana guides me to Hapatoni, among the most magnificent sights of the Marquesas. Here a long and ancient grassy alley runs parallel to the beach under coconut palms. It lies between a long succession of *paepaes,* stone terraces on which the Marquesans built their houses.

Here a man invites us to share a meal of fish, wild chicken, and cold *popoi,* or breadfruit paste. The ancient Marquesans, constantly exposed to wars and famines, stored popoi in huge leaf-lined pits. Now people store it thus in small amounts, to let it ferment. A dab of this adds tang to fresh popoi. One has to be Marquesan to appreciate it, I conclude.

I must leave Tahuata by speedboat—the taxi of the Marquesas today—to catch the weekly plane from Atuona to Ua Pu, next island on my route. In July, unfortunately, the sea is rough on any day, and often worse. The speedboat trip takes only an hour, but over the mad billows of the Bordelais Channel, a narrow corridor between Tahuata and Hiva Oa. Here waters that have gained unchallenged speed in their long race from South America must suddenly meet waves surging back from the coasts.

The waves heave us up and drop us and drench us. The pilot speeds up to avoid the biggest ones and slows down as we drop in seemingly bottomless hollows. Sometimes he cannot muster enough power from his motor to pull us over these mountains of water; he must veer horizontally below the crest. Off Teaehoa Point he almost loses control of the boat. Coming from every direction, the waves toss it about like a nutshell and almost swamp it twice. If the motor fails, they will break us on the rocks, for the pilot runs close inshore. Marquesans do this to limit the swimming distance in case of shipwreck—thus increasing the risk of capsizing. But soon we are in normal sea again. Heavy, but predictable, sea.

On the islet Motu Manu, young Antonio Lichtle from Ua Huka climbs to gather sooty tern eggs from a rookery. The author explains the tricky approach: "Our pilot brought us near the cliff, and standing on the boat's prow, we each caught the rope at the perfect instant, lest the sea smash us on the rocks." Above, one parent guards its single egg while others bully the harvesters.

With volcanic towers, pinnacles, and spires, Ua Pu emerges from sea and clouds like a fairy castle. No forests shroud its valleys, for it lies in the rain shadow of its sister islands, but it will provide incidents as varied as those of a folk tale.

On the landing strip, a young man in a jeep radios to the French pilot the speed of the wind, often too strong for landing. Then he drives up and down the strip to keep 23 horses off of it. He takes me down to the village of Hakahau, where his mother, a sturdy matron called Rosalie, will give me *pension*—room and board.

She serves the meals at one end of a large terrace, by a big color TV set that attracts thirty or forty viewers every night. At the other end stands a small altar, with two statuettes of the Virgin Mary garlanded with flowers and shells. Here at 6 a.m. the family prays for half an hour each morning.

Every house in Hakahau seems to display such a shrine. So strong is Roman Catholicism in the Marquesas that some have called this group "the Spain of Polynesia," and in Ua Pu the French priest is especially active.

Now Hakahau is preparing for Bastille Day. Four wooden structures are rising next to the town hall, to house restaurants and a ballroom.

Taporo II arrives, and stirs a burst of excitement. A dinghy shuttle runs to the quay, where a jeep shuttle takes over: canned goods, wine, soap, a bicycle—all the necessities of modern life. Then the jeep brings copra for the schooner to take to market. A French couple tell me that if two or even three schooners arrive at the same time, a mad competition for copra begins. Rumors are spread, destinations become secret, and passengers are accepted for one island when the boat will go to another.

Bastille Day comes at last. As I sit eating dinner, a man who has already celebrated freely comes up shouting that he wants a word with the stranger. Rosalie rebukes him. He insists. She fends him off. He comes back. I am amused, but Rosalie loses patience. She strides up to him, lifts him in her arms, carries him to the street, and dumps him on his face. The TV viewers cheer. I think it tactful to slip away.

As I stroll down to the town hall, another drunk approaches me.

"You look German," he says. "Heil Hitler! Could you then explain to me what Hitler meant by 'To be or not to be'?"

I tell him that he has his authors mixed up, and leave him cogitating.

Inside the ballroom, colored lights and blaring American music seem to make the girls shyer than ever. They refuse to leave their benches; the boys, undaunted, dance together. Outside, children and dogs enjoy themselves tremendously. The children are fascinated by the glitter, the unusual festivity. The dogs sniff the air eagerly; I watch four of them nibble at the meat of a brochette vendor absorbed by the dancers' antics. By ten o'clock even the girls are dancing. More people are coming in all the time. And everyone greets me with surprising warmth. It seems appropriate, on this fairy-tale castle of an island, that people should throw off their deep reserve for one night in the year.

On Ua Huka, least populous of the inhabited islands, my host is Leon Lichtle, mayor and delegate to the Territorial Assembly, and he guides me through its valleys with outspoken pride. He takes me on foot to Haavei, which belongs to his family, explaining on the way that he has refused to install electricity—except for the village generator—because families would skimp to buy expensive appliances. "The first to suffer when belts are tightened are always the children. But electricity will come soon now; I cannot resist any more."

We find his parents, his brother's family and his own, with a couple of nieces, preparing to roast a pig Polynesian style. All night they will keep a fire burning over volcanic stones until they grow red hot. Meanwhile we dine on sea urchins, raw fish, lobster, algae cooked in coconut milk, poached breadfruit, roasted bananas, bread baked in leaves—all delicious. Then the teenagers go off to the beach while Leon's father tells me the family story. "We like to travel," he concludes. "Every two years we visit a different country. We have seen North and South America, Europe, Australia. But we would not trade this valley for any place in the world."

Next morning the cooks crisscross green twigs over the hot stones. On these they set meat wrapped in leaves, along with bananas, and a closed pot containing the liver and heart. They cover the whole with banana leaves, then with wet sacks, then with sand. Unearthed after a couple of hours, the warm pork falls apart at the touch and melts in the mouth. And then the men go fishing, the women and girls gather small shells on the beach to thread into garlands, and I return to the village of Vaipaee to join a man from the Society Islands on a horse-buying expedition.

"I need a dozen horses to start a riding school," he says. "On Ua Huka there are many, but they are not easy to buy." In three hours' walk up Hane Valley, we indeed see many horses wandering among low green bushes, but the men of Hane are not in the mood for business. They are still celebrating "the July"—as Marquesans call Bastille Day. "Come back tomorrow," they say. My companion is philosophical. "They claim that all those horses have owners," he tells me. "But Leon tries all the time to find out who owns those horses that stray onto the airstrip. He would fine them. Everyone says those horses are wild!"

The sooty terns prove wild indeed when Leon takes me to see the rookery on a cliff-rimmed islet offshore. The adults defend their eggs with fury. They deafen us with shrill cries, peck at our skulls, shower us with excrement. And I see a strange variant of flight as we finally clamber down the access rope: In the clear water, raising and lowering their "wings," glide several manta rays, dark as basalt and larger than grand pianos.

By plane I reach Terre Déserte, a barren area on Nuku Hiva, last and largest of the islands on my route. The cross-island road has been blocked by landslides, and I resolve to go by horseback to Taiohae, the main village and administrative center, on the southern shore. A young man called Maurice is assigned to guide me, but I have to organize a kind of amateur roundup to get our horses. We lasso one in twenty minutes; with a jeep, and many misadventures, we track the second through the scrub for two hours. Both are so spooky when we set out that we lead them up sun-baked slopes. Maurice looks downtrodden; I try to cheer him up, with no success; he seems unable to speak.

We ride for three hours up eroded valleys before we enter lush highland country where a great cool wind whistles in our ears. I dismount to take pictures, saying, "Lead my horse—I'll catch up with you. Go slow." I work for an hour, then walk uphill and run downhill after him. Sometimes I see him afar, riding steadily on. At dusk, in cold and heavy mist, I cross a final ridge; I find him sitting motionless in a small shed, our bread and cheese spread untasted on a dirty cardboard box. I want to talk things out, but he disarms me with a wan smile. We eat in silence.

Within minutes Maurice is snoring on the ground. A thunderstorm, the clatter of rain on the metal roof, the gusts of wind are powerless against his sleep. As are the water leaking through the roof and the rats chasing each other over our luggage and our bodies. I do not sleep so well.

Next morning a crisis, in steady rain. Our horses bolt, with all my money and all my exposed film. Whatever I say, Maurice just stares blankly, pathetic as a wet puppy, so I talk to myself. We catch our mounts after a wet farce of a struggle. Before long, Maurice's horse slips and tumbles under him; he gets up, a shapeless length of mud. Still, not an oath, not a word. And I start to grow fond of him.

In sunlight at last we cross green plateau, broad meadows and pine groves; we descend along majestic ramparts, always in silence. Unannounced, the shining bay of Taiohae comes into view, two great rocky sentinels guarding the entrance, yachts at anchor in the peaceful circle of water. Nuku Hiva, I decide, is surely the most sublime island of all.

I find the best lodging yet in Taiohae, at an inn managed by two Americans, Frank and Rose Corser. I see the bay of Anaho, fit for paradise. I visit the valley of Taipivai, unique in beauty, and understand why it inspired Herman Melville to make it immortal in his novel *Typee*. And my cheerful young guide Thomas, who knows Maurice, clears up one minor mystery. "He's a really nice guy," says Thomas. "But how did you communicate with him?" "What do you mean? He consistently refused to talk with me!" Thomas laughs. "But how could he, if he does not speak French?" Too late I remember Tehaumate's worries about boys who drop out of school. Now I begin to appreciate the true remoteness of this world.

The Marquesas are so small, so far. The blue of the sky merges with the blue of the sea all around. I recall these isles with fondness—shall I ever return?

Faithful tradition lives in the wood sculptures of Damien Haturau, as he carves a Last Supper scene for a church on Ua Pu. Most Marquesan youths carve, in local woods; they learn by watching and imitating fathers or uncles. In the forests of Hiva Oa stand weathered, lichen-covered tikis, images of deified ancestors and other gods fashioned in lava rock by island sculptors some five centuries ago.

"We would not trade this valley for any place in the world," says patriarch Joseph Lichtle. The family has owned Ua Huka's Haavei Valley since Joseph's parents came to the Marquesas from Alsace in the late 1800s. Above, his son Leon descends the steps of the vacation bungalow he built. As one of two Marquesan delegates to the Territorial Assembly and mayor of his island, Leon works to protect Polynesian elements of life on Ua Huka—home to 350 of the 6,000 Marquesans and least populous of the six inhabited isles. Out for a ride, Leon's son, Antonio-Maheatete, and his bearded friend Vetea Hart watch three generations of Lichtle women gather shells for necklaces and bathroom ornaments.

23

Cloak of green drapes Fatu Hiva's Omoa Valley, typical of the sheltered glens where Marquesans first settled. Equipped for a new land, seafaring Polynesians carried food stock in their outrigger canoes, bringing pigs, dogs, and chickens to the Marquesas. Europeans added horses, goats, sheep, and cattle (right), which run wild; these charged the author, then turned away.

OVERLEAF: *Free as the sailing bird above, a surefooted wild horse grazes the plunging volcanic slopes of Fatu Hiva's Hanavave Valley.*

Feast for a dreamer's eyes, haven for a world-weary soul: Waves roll across dark sands and worn stones in the Bay of Puamau on Hiva Oa. Marquesan vistas have always inspired artists, writers, romantics, and refugees from a more complicated world. A valley on Nuku Hiva provided the setting for Herman Melville's novel Typee; in his travel book In The South Seas Robert Louis Stevenson wrote that "Few men who come to the islands leave them; they grow grey where they alighted; the palm shades and the trade-wind fans them till they die. . . ." In an overgrown cemetery near Atuona stand the gravestones of two who stayed. French post-Impressionist Paul Gauguin left Tahiti and spent his last two years painting on Hiva Oa, and Belgian singer-composer Jacques Brel, who lived in the Marquesas for years as a voluntary exile, asked to be buried on the island he called "my paradise."

29

When the ships come in, excitement stirs the village of Taiohae on Nuku Hiva, administrative headquarters and chief port of call for the Marquesas. Showers mist the hills above Taiohae Bay, where two cargo vessels lie at anchor. The larger, Taporo III, brings goods from Tahiti for transshipment to smaller Taporo II, which carries imports and passengers among the Marquesas. All goods bound for the group arrive by such ships, still referred to locally as "copra schooners"; the term harks back to the 19th century, when copra—dried coconut meat—provided the mainstay of European trade in the Pacific. In the Marquesas, copra remains the principal export. By Nuku Hiva's Anaho Bay, a woman spreads copra to dry.

*Days pass at a free and breezy pace on Hiva Oa, where a home in the
village of Puamau shows the Marquesan preference for modern housing.
Near the heart of most settlements stands a Catholic church, revealing the
strength of that faith in islands sometimes called the "Spain of Polynesia."
In Atuona, boys test the spirit of their fighting cocks, trained to capture wild
chickens in the forests. A young man cradles his feathered warrior with pride
(opposite); a string leash will help the bird entangle a chicken for the
dinner table. The author's friend Aroma says of the playful hunt,
"Who but boys would go through so much trouble for so small a reward?"*

32

Along an alley trod by the ancients, a boy of the Tahuata village of Hapatoni rides between rows of raised paepaes, *stone platforms built by the Marquesans as foundations for homes, temples, and ceremonial sites. Until this century, many islanders still lived in houses made of airy bamboo walls and coconut-leaf thatched roofs, constructed atop old stone terraces. Swaying palms line the rocky beach at Hapatoni (opposite), framing a view of the horizon where ships sailing from the west may pass. The Polynesians who reached Marquesan shores carried the fruits, nuts, and roots to grow many plants now considered typical of South Seas isles, including breadfruit, pandanus, and the graceful coconut palm.*

OVERLEAF: *Sunbeams stream through roiling clouds, illuminating the village of Vaitahu on Tahuata, where the French claimed possession of the Marquesas. A red-roofed Catholic church crowns the village. As in many Marquesan settlements, the church probably rises from the site of a pagan ceremonial plaza. Forested mountains dwarf the tiny village, a vista expressing Melville's sentiments for the Marquesas when he wrote in* Typee: *"Very often when lost in admiration at its beauty, I have experienced a pang of regret that a scene so enchanting should be hidden from the world in these remote seas, and seldom meet the eyes of devoted lovers of nature."*

Northern Afghanistan

By Jane R. McCauley
Photographs by Roland and Sabrina Michaud

A pallid, deathly hue coats the land as if nature had been draining its strength for thousands of years. From time to time, the wind stirs, its low, mournful wail sweeping across the broad earth. Far to the south, the vast plains break gently into wave after wave of rose-hued hills. A haze of sultry heat hangs over their naked slopes. Suddenly, in the reddish light of a slowly sinking sun, the thin, angular column of a caravan emerges. Obscured by billowing dust, it drifts in and out of visibility.

Under the sparse shade of a lone willow tree, two figures stand motionless and ponder the dreamlike vision. In this aura of mystery and magic, their minds are carried back to that age of caliphs and caravans.

"It seemed like a memory from *One Thousand and One Nights*," Roland and Sabrina Michaud agreed. "We went there to follow in the paths of the caravans, to adjust our lives to the slow, mesmerizing pace of the camels." In their apartment in Paris, they were telling me about their first trip across the northern plains of Afghanistan. A journey that impelled them to return often during the next 14 years. I listened intently to their words, chosen with great care in English.

"In our compact Austrian jeep—'Zasie'—we plodded west to east across this immeasurable land," said Roland. "Each day brought new challenges." Their voices overlapped with examples: "a blinding snowstorm stinging our skins like a swarm of bees . . . rainstorms that left us swimming through an ocean of mud . . . foot-wide ruts blocking our path."

"And always there was the dust," Roland continued. "Swirling and drifting, it mantled the countryside like freshly fallen snow. The prickly spines of the desert plants attracted it like magnets. Coating our bodies, the fine grains oozed through every pore, effacing every feature."

In a faraway time those hardy men known as cameleers battled these same elements. The main east-west trade routes crisscrossed on these plains. Like the gnarled branches of a tree, byways of the great Silk Road fanned out across them. Along these sinuous trails, in mud or dust, caravans picked their way westward from China through the lofty passes of the Pamirs. With them they carried elegant silks, brocades, jade, and porcelains. They traveled in the cooling breezes of evening, or in winter, the pale moonlight and heaven's jewels overhead their only guides.

The cameleers' arduous route took them across deserts and mountains and through the chain of oasis towns that dot the countryside like a broken necklace of emeralds: Kholm, Mazar-e-Sharif, Balkh. Eventually, most found their way to Persia and from there to the ports of the Mediterranean.

In the weathered face of Mahmad-Niyaz, photographer Roland Michaud saw
"the passionate independence, pride, courtesy, and dignity of the Afghans." Until his
death in 1977, Mahmad made donkey saddles in the bazaar of Tashkurghan.

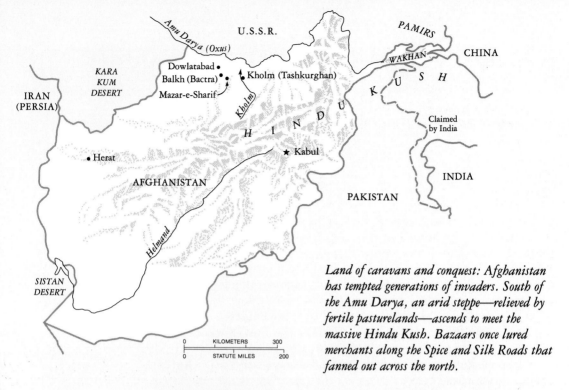

Land of caravans and conquest: Afghanistan has tempted generations of invaders. South of the Amu Darya, an arid steppe—relieved by fertile pasturelands—ascends to meet the massive Hindu Kush. Bazaars once lured merchants along the Spice and Silk Roads that fanned out across the north.

Meanwhile, caravans brought wares from Rome and Sicily: jewels, gold, linens, and woolens. Along the southern artery from India came indigo, spices, and cotton goods. In exchange, traders could offer lapis lazuli mined in Afghanistan, cherished by kings for four thousand years.

It was these brave souls and romantic sagas of the land they crossed that lured Roland and Sabrina in the first place. In their wanderings they found reminders of those bygone days when they stopped for a night's rest in the oasis towns or paused to refresh themselves in teahouses.

Now the Michauds were sharing their memories with me. Often, as we talked in the midst of hundreds of slides of their travels, we thought with sadness about the oppression and warfare that plague Afghanistan today. Where caravans once traveled, Soviet tanks and soldiers now tread, filling mountain passes and village streets. On a late December night in 1979, a Soviet airlift began to ferry combat units southward across the border. While much of the Western world was celebrating Christmas, Afghanistan lay stricken. Within weeks, the Soviets had installed a new government, replacing a floundering Marxist regime that had seized power in 1978. Men of the Red Army found themselves fighting the poorly armed but implacable guerrillas who call themselves *mujahidin,* holy warriors of Islam.

And so this country that has struggled valiantly since its birth to resist invaders finds itself again at war. For me to journey through this land was impossible. So I sought those who have spent time in the mythical caravan cities of the north, rubbed shoulders in the millennia-old bazaars, and gossiped with its hardy, rough-hewn people. Through them, I would re-create this enigmatic land as it was in the years before the invasion. Through them, I would gain insights into its people.

"You must understand what distinguishes the north from the south," an Afghan scholar once told me. "There is a lack of militarism in the north, and the people are more friendly and less aggressive." Yet peace has seldom prevailed here. Since the dawn of civilization, armies have ranged over the region that offered avenues to China, India, and the disputed northern lands eventually taken by the Tsars. To control these passes meant not only new conquests but limiting the expansion of rival powers as well.

Among the first conquerors to traverse the north's difficult terrain was Alexander the Great. After subduing neighboring Persia and crossing the Sistan Desert, he headed north. With his army of 30,000, he fought his way through the snowbound, icy passes of the Hindu Kush on to the plains. By 329 B.C. the north's main cities had fallen.

He established his base at Bactra, later called Balkh, a place so splendid that admiring Arabs would name it "Mother of Cities." Despite repeated episodes of destruction it prospered until the 1860s as the north's political capital, a religious center, and the main depot for goods carried by the caravans. Alexander's men held it nearly two years before he moved on to India, leaving a profound influence on the arts of the north.

Thereafter, power passed through the hands of Greeks, Persians, and Turks. An Arab invasion brought Islam to Balkh in 653. This new religion spread slowly here, with a decisive Arab victory in 715 securing its influence. Since that time, it has dominated the law and customs of the country.

Conquest and an effort to check the power of Islam brought the fierce Mongol Genghis Khan in 1220. With his army of 100,000 Tartars, he razed every building from Balkh eastward. Men, women, and children were led onto the open plain and put to the sword. Prosperity did not return again until the 15th century under Tamerlane's successors.

"Perhaps this area has known more invasions than any other place," Professor Jack Shroder commented to me in his office at the University of Nebraska in Omaha. He was in the midst of preparing a comprehensive atlas of Afghanistan. "But it is geography that has been one of the real constraints. Mountains stretch across the south and east, and lowlands on the north. Then there's a desert to the west, really awesome."

Lands of astonishing variety, the northern plains lie southeast of the U.S.S.R.'s Kara Kum Desert and west of the Wakhan Corridor, which projects through the ranges of the Pamirs into Chinese Turkistan. To the north, the Amu Darya flows nearly 800 miles between snow peaks or salt flats to form a natural boundary with the U.S.S.R. Alexander knew this river as the Oxus. Its narrow, winding channels spread like lesser arteries from the great, between low crumbling banks and high mud cliffs. Between unyielding deserts of stone and sand, fields of cotton, corn, barley, and wheat flourish. Through them runs a labyrinth of irrigation canals lined by hardy tamarisk trees. Rich pasturelands pattern the countryside, a mosaic of mossy greens, earthy browns, and golden yellows.

"The soil in places here is—with irrigation—some of the most fertile in the world," Dr. Shroder told me. "We have the same kind here on the Great Plains. This fine, powdery loess, as it is called, sprinkles like glitter from the sky. It can form hills like haystacks hundreds of feet high." He spoke with the same enthusiasm as the others who had visited the area.

Along the Amu Darya's plains, shepherds accompanied by scruffy dogs tend flocks of karakul sheep. From them come the prized skins of the newborns called astrakhan, or Persian lamb.

Some distance to the south, wild pistachios, barberries, pomegranates, and roses thrive on the gently undulating slopes of the foothills of the Hindu Kush. For millennia this formidable range has been a cultural as well as a political barrier between northern and southern Afghanistan.

"These mountains have affected the climate, too," Dr. Shroder remarked one afternoon. "The monsoons can't cross them, but the rains fill the streams and flash floods dump water across the plains. Then, too, the cold winds blowing out of Siberia are trapped by them on the plains.

"One of the most active earthquake zones in the world," he continued, "reaches across the eastern half of the steppe into the U.S.S.R. and China. As the subcontinent of India pushes into Central Asia, the Hindu Kush mountains are thrusting upward." As early as 818, travelers in Balkh saw its walls toppled by massive tremors. In 1948 a substantial quake leveled much of Mazar-e-Sharif and was felt throughout the north.

A journey across this area was slow and hazardous. Most caravans could travel no more than one *serai,* between ten and twenty-five miles a day. Merchants desperately searched for faster, more economical transport. By the early 16th century, trade began shifting from these toilsome overland routes to blue water. The seas for all their perils seemed easier than the craggy passes of Central Asia. East-west traffic on the Silk Road declined.

Yet some caravans remained. Even today—with the rutted trails usually replaced by paved roads—local caravans carrying bales of cotton or stalks of *buta* sway along beside lorries. "And the way of life fashioned by the cameleers lingers on," Roland remarked one evening. "The unhurried traveler could still catch a glimpse of that long-ago era in the small forgotten towns where caravans used to stop." On the dust-choked paths, the wayfarer had to contend with arduous terrain, ill-tempered camels, and roving bands of thieves. The towns offered him a welcome respite. There he found food and rest, news and entertainment, and trade—the most essential thing. Perhaps it was just yesterday the caravans left one of these towns where the threads of that era have endured longer than any others in the north.

Richly hued chadris *conceal both face and figure for women of Tashkurghan. Custom kept these garments in use in smaller towns years after ladies in the capital discarded them, in 1959. At right, two silks display the antique patterns produced by a process of dyeing called* ikat. *Traders and immigrants from Bukhara brought this technique into the area, with the memory of certain designs.*

Kholm was a cameleer's dream two hundred years ago. This oasis town sat at the crossroads of major trade routes, the most prosperous city of the north. Its commercial sphere extended as far west as the Mediterranean.

Clusters of domed mud dwellings greet the visitor to the town that lies about a day's ride by camel from the modern provincial capital of Mazar-e-Sharif. Behind mud walls, red and pink roses, a favorite of Kholm, grow abundantly in serene gardens. Here, in flickering shadows and cool shade, the Afghans find a reprieve from summer's 105° temperature. Beyond these paradises, lush orchards of almond and apricot flourish before melting into neatly aligned patchwork squares of wheat and barley.

A centuries-old camel trail leads northward past salt flats to the murky waters of the Amu Darya. Along the northern banks, a barbed-wire fence zigzags through the swamplike perimeter lands of the U.S.S.R.

To the south, a massive brick castle commands the entrance to the Tangi-Tashkurghan gorge. A narrow paved road eases through the 1,000-

foot solid rock walls and tumbles into the town. In the late 1700s, this imposing entrance proved an ideal place to levy taxes on arriving caravans.

In 1964 officials changed the town's name from Tashkurghan, or Stone Fort in Turkic, to Kholm, probably of Persian origin. But the people cling tenaciously to the unofficial name. The defense of cherished traditions is important here, and this is one of the things that captivated Roland and Sabrina when they first found the town. "To us," they commented one afternoon, "Tashkurghan is the pearl of Afghanistan." They talked about the people. "We found them more happy, more serene, and more pleasant than most of our countrymen. Their manners were so civilized that sometimes we felt as though we were barbarians."

I thought about their remarks a few weeks later when I met Aman. He wanted to be known simply as Aman. An Afghan from Tashkurghan, he, perhaps better than anyone, could give me insights into this unique place. His memories of the town are some of the happiest of his life. He told me about one, an impression from childhood.

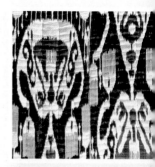

"Tashkurghan has three important fruits—almonds, pomegranates, and figs. When the almond trees blossomed, their sweet smells perfumed the air for miles around. It seemed to drift on clouds in the evening's breezes. I would climb a hillside, and the town below, bathed in moonlight, looked like a field of fluffy white snow."

Aman's heritage reflects the cultural and ethnic threads interwoven here. "My father, who was district governor for several years, was a Tajik. My mother is Pashtun. So, you see," he laughed, "I'm half and half."

Tashkurghan has always remained culturally and ethnically mixed. As foreigners filled its market, the town absorbed elements of the Persian, Turkic, and Chinese cultures. Today, the dominant groups are the Tajik, of Persian origin and probably the oldest identifiable in the area, and the Uzbeks, who trace their descent from Russian Turkistan. In the 19th century, a few Pashtuns settled here also, at the king's behest.

About eight miles north of the town, a mound of ruins climbs a steep hillside. Here, the original Kholm, predecessor to Tashkurghan, was founded in the seventh century. Mir Qilich Ali Beg, who ruled the area from 1787 to 1817, is credited with establishing the town on its present site. Local legend says the town was moved upstream to save it from repeated floods. Probably the move was a tactical one, however. By the late 1840s, Kabul was extending its power northward and favoring the pilgrimage town Mazar-e-Sharif (the Exalted Shrine). Mazar became the dominant city of the north. Tashkurghan remained, however, an important commercial center, dealing in livestock and leather, fabrics and fruit.

"This town was very well situated for trade," Dr. Pierre Centlivres told me one rainy afternoon in Neuchâtel, Switzerland. In this lakefront town ringed by the Jura Mountains, he and his wife, Micheline, often reminisce about their year and a half in Tashkurghan. As anthropologists, the Centlivres had undertaken an intensive study of the town and its ethnic groups. As I stood at the window of their home watching clouds drift across the mountains, I thought how different these jagged peaks seem to the gently rolling loess foothills that lie to the south of Tashkurghan.

"A north-south road," Dr. Centlivres continued, "ran from Shikarpur—in Pakistan—through Kabul, Tashkurghan, Balkh, and to Bukhara. And then there was the east-west road that ran through Herat, across

Turkistan, and into China. These roads met in the town. I'm talking about the end of the 1700s and the beginning of the 1800s."

For the Centlivres, Tashkurghan is traditional Asia, a traditional way of life. As we sipped steaming cups of tea and nibbled on delightful Swiss chocolates, they talked about the way they were welcomed into the homes. I recognized in what they said the same enthusiastic response to the people that I had seen in the Michauds.

"The people are very kind here. But it is not just that. It's a generous hospitality system with obligations. It has rules, and you must respect

Shafts of sunlight illumine the last covered bazaar of northern Afghanistan. At right, rug merchants await customers in the imposing tim *at the market's center. Shoppers (above) browse among open-front shops under the shelter of a wood-beamed roof.*

them. I may eat at your house tonight, but that doesn't mean you must eat at my house one month from now. It just means someone will." I was reminded of a statement in Mountstuart Elphinstone's 19th-century classic *Kingdom of Caubul:* "One of the most remarkable characteristics of the Afghauns is their hospitality." He noted that "a man who travelled over the whole country without money would never be in want of a meal."

Later that day, the Centlivres showed me the beautiful handiwork they had acquired in Tashkurghan. A few of the finer pieces had come as wedding gifts. Although they were married in Switzerland, they told me, the people of the town held a feast in their honor at the time of the ceremony.

The delicately embroidered caps, silk coats, and handkerchiefs showed some of the finest needlecraft I've ever seen. Each tiny stitch of silk thread lay evenly against the fabric. Carefully, I lifted an exquisite lappet from a *chapan,* or silk coat, lined with batting. Vertical stripes of pink, yellow, and green ran through the fabric. I ran my hand over the smooth stitches along the front, those used in crewel. "Look inside," Micheline urged. I saw the inside as skillfully embroidered as the front.

"The silk in this coat was dyed by a very complicated technique called *ikat,*" Micheline told me. This sophisticated method, not unlike tie dyeing, was introduced from Bukhara. "The fine threads are carefully wrapped together and dipped in large basins of dye. Before they are placed on the loom, the bundles of threads are dyed again, one by one, beginning with the darkest." Although the manufacture of such fabrics was never a major industry in Tashkurghan, they became a significant commodity for traders from Bukhara and Samarkand.

For the women of Tashkurghan, handiwork brings a bit of income and a welcome pastime. While their children play nearby, women stitch the round caps worn by boys and men under turbans. Each region has a distinctive pattern. Between household chores, they often make candies for their children to sell in the bazaar. In this Muslim land, even the high-walled gardens reflect the female's life of seclusion.

"The women are like jewels that are hidden," Sabrina remarked as we strolled in a grassy park one crisp afternoon. "Without an introduction, it is impossible to meet them." After many weeks in Tashkurghan, she had received invitations into a few homes, a compliment in this area where

the privacy of women is sacrosanct. Around sundown, a few shrouded figures may stroll the streets to visit a friend or stop at a shrine to pray. Older
women may wander with some freedom. But the younger ones never appear in teahouses and seldom enter the crowded bazaar.

As the early morning heat slowly ascends on the parched steppe, bus-
tling crowds begin to fill the narrow, winding mud streets of Tashkurghan's bazaar. The ancient mud-brick footbridge joining the town's main
districts carries a procession of cameleers. Using crudely hewn canes of
poplar to steady themselves, they coax their stubborn donkeys and haughty

camels. The animals—sometimes adorned with brightly embroidered
sacking—carry cumbersome loads of dried buta. This plant of the steppe, a
relative of tumbleweed, is burned for fuel.

The merchants, their pale faces withered like apricots, sit crosslegged
in front of their shops. "Peace be upon thee," one cries out to a passerby.
Another: "Are you well?" The phrases of greeting vary little. Whirling a
cylindrical pot, a dervish chants to chase away evil spirits. Shoppers reward
him with what they can afford: two oranges, a piece of bread, a few coins.
Donkeys bray. Partridges cackle. Abacuses rattle.

This teeming marketplace functioned as the most important commercial center of the north before the 1870s. Then, buyers and sellers roamed
the maze of alleyways that twist through the heart of the town. Then—and
perhaps now—merchants would carry news of changing fashions, newly
chosen officials, feuding neighbors, and the latest fighting.

Rising above the muddy streets, the dome-roofed *tim* stands at the core
of market activity. This stately structure, of durable kiln-fired brick, once
housed moneychangers as well as prestigious merchants, the vendors of
imported merchandise. In the muffled quiet and semi-dark rooms, they

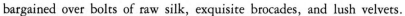

bargained over bolts of raw silk, exquisite brocades, and lush velvets.

Like the spokes of a wagonwheel, the streets of the marketplace radiate from the River Kholm. The slow, rhythmic pounding of blacksmiths' hammers fills one passageway, while another glows with the fires of coppersmiths shaping their gleaming water jugs. Bolts of cloth—a rainbow of purples, saffrons, blues, and lemon yellows—fill the shops of another area. A succession of scents—bread baking, fried liver and onions, skewered lamb, animal dung—assails the nostrils.

For more than a century, this busy mart prospered. But with World War I came the closing of the border and a swift end to trade with Russian Turkistan. New roads were built, roads that bypassed Tashkurghan to favor other towns. Trade shifted from international to regional. New products arrived; some crafts disappeared; others changed.

"It was during those decades," Dr. Centlivres told me, "that roofs on bazaar streets were torn down. Until then, most of the bazaars of the north were covered. Tashkurghan has remained as the last covered bazaar in the north. The town was declining in commercial importance, and so the bazaar was not destroyed." Many of these roofs, of wooden slats underlined with matted reeds, have been lost to age, weather, new construction, or the demands of commercial lorries and military vehicles. But in the cool shade and subtle lighting of those that remain, it is easy to understand why they were built in the first place.

Away from the flow of transient travelers close to the river, craftsmen turn out intricately carved woodwork, silver bracelets and rings set with deep red carnelians, and delicate wicker cages. In this ancient covered section of the bazaar, the exchanging of social pleasantries is as important as the price obtained. Here, time is marked only by the serene cry of the muezzin as he summons men to prayer five times a day.

At his call, the rap of the hammer ceases; the craftsmen kneel in their shops and turn their faces to Mecca. In this land where "every moment is imbued with religion," as a perceptive stranger has said, art is a spiritual discipline. Each trade has its spiritual patron. To avert envy and show that only God is perfect, an Afghan will include a small defect in his work. One day as I sat in the Michaud apartment, a blue-and-white porcelain vase on the mantel caught my eye. Sunlight streaming through a window revealed thin metal bands across cracks in the vase. Roland explained that it had been repaired by a *patragar,* or china mender. These craftsmen once roamed throughout all the bazaars of Afghanistan. With a glue of lime and egg, the vase had been cemented, then reinforced with the metal strips.

"An Afghan says, 'The foot is the master,'" Roland continued, showing me how the china mender holds the object between his feet and with a surgeon's precision drills tiny holes. An ordinary record-player needle, or perhaps a pin, is fitted in the drill. I could easily understand why this craft flourished in a land where every penny counts.

I was curious about just how Roland had obtained the vase. Among Afghans bargaining is customary—in fact, almost a courtesy. He told me that after tea and conversation with a young merchant one day, he asked if he would sell the vase. A few moments later the young man replied, "Oh, it has too much value." "The day you will sell it for ten times less," Roland answered him, "you let me know."

"Bargaining is difficult for Westerners to understand," he remarked. "It's not just a question of money, but of respecting the craftsman's work."

"And when did you finally get the vase?" I asked him. "Three years later," he replied with a sheepish grin.

Intermediaries, or third parties, often assist in transactions of more valuable items such as astrakhan pelts. To hasten or seal the bargain, an intermediary will take the hands of the parties involved and bring them together. Bystanders watch with the interest of connoisseurs.

Of all the crafts of Tashkurghan (they number three score and ten), perhaps woodworking has gained the largest reputation. In their dim, tiny shops, wood turners fashion handsome cradles of willow wood and bedposts, each a barbershop pole of yellows, oranges, blues, and reds. The colors, imported as powders from India and Pakistan, are mixed with melted wax and poured into wooden molds. Then the man holds the crayon-like hardened color against the post as the lathe turns it.

Across the river a little way from the crafts section, vendors hawk their wares in the onion and rice markets. The fruit merchants stack their apples—polished with a cloth until they gleam—into precise pyramids. "*Yak-rupia! Yak-rupia!*—One afghani per piece!"

Just beyond this section, buyers and sellers gather in teahouses at the close of the morning's business to refresh themselves with steaming tea. In summer they sip bowls of refreshing Chinese green tea; in winter, the warming Indian black tea. Nowadays, in these establishments that arose during the caravan era, record players blare Pakistani or Indian tunes. Amid the bubbling of their water pipes, men discuss local affairs and market prices: "Has your bazaar been hot?" Conversations may also run to the next partridge fight, an event that lures spectators much as weekend football does elsewhere.

The white-throated chukars, or partridges, are seen throughout Tashkurghan. Shopkeepers hang their domed wicker cages in storefronts, and the birds amble at leisure among customers in teahouses. Clipped wings prevent them from flying.

At dawn on the sunbaked clay floor of the town's ancient citadel, the Bala Hissar, a crowd of blue-turbaned men add their voices to the cheerful cacophony of the partridges. With the blast of a whistle, the owners crouch beside their cages and release the birds for a brief trial of strength—never of bloodshed.

"The training of these birds is rigorous," Roland explained to me one morning. "The master compels his birds to jump off rocks to strengthen their muscles. Look, I'll show you!" Crouching, with his head tilted, he hopped from a small footstool to the floor. And after my burst of laughter subsided, I thought about the contrast between the formidable character of these men and the gentleness they show their birds.

In hot weather, to keep their favorites in fighting trim, men carry the cages to the riverbank and the water's refreshing breezes. A hearty diet of apricot kernels in summer and wheat in winter, with protection from winter's chill, keeps them healthy. In a land where mere survival is a constant

"Like jewels that are hidden"—the photographer's words convey the obscure, yet rich, life of Afghan women. In a rare moment of leisure, a young matron embroiders a round cap worn by men under turbans; the cap's distinctive pattern identifies the region of Tashkurghan. Although attitudes and roles have changed in the past 20 years, women in more isolated areas remain obedient to custom; typically, they eat apart from men, and rarely appear outside the bounds of home. Under her mother's tutelage, little Turpekai will learn the ways of women; eventually she may grow up to marry a man that her family chooses for her.

SABRINA MICHAUD/RAPHO

47

struggle, the care and the food lavished on these birds seem incongruous.

As summer's intense heat fades into winter's biting chill, so changes have come to this traditional bazaar. On Main Street, the high-rent district north of the craft section, tea merchants and tailors work alongside repairmen who fix bicycles and transistor radios. A few glassfront shops have appeared. Other stores have moved to the perimeters to be closer to the trade that wanders off the nearby highway. Some crafts—gunsmiths, cloth-printers—have disappeared. Others—the skills of the coppersmiths, silversmiths, and leatherworkers—are dying out. Whenever imports make it cheaper to replace breakables than to repair them, china menders, too, will surely become rare.

In 1978 Roland Michaud returned to Tashkurghan. One morning as he leafed through the pages of his diary, he told me about his visit.

"I thought it would have changed more. The old gardener—the *baba*—was still in charge of the hotel. He seemed to have grown younger. Some people had disappeared. My good friend Jumakhan, the caravansary keeper, had died. The earthquake that struck in 1976 had damaged some places. Most were not rebuilt. But the bazaar . . . it is still unique and strangely beautiful. My eyes, ears, nose, and heart were captured again." He paused for some moments as though lost in thought. Finally, he spoke.

"Perhaps the bazaar does not exist now," Roland pondered, his eyes brimming with tears. "But you cannot kill a spiritual atmosphere as quickly as you kill a man."

I would like to visit this land someday. To walk its harsh desert, sweat in its intense heat, and feel the bite of its winds. To those who shared their experiences with me, I am grateful. There are others I would like to have talked with, but understandably they are reluctant as the guerrillas in their country continue to fight on.

Of those I spoke with throughout my journey, each one holds certain memories of Tashkurghan, its fascinating bazaar, and the vast plains. For some there's a magic in the sweep of open country; for others it's the sweet smell of the almond blossoms in the night's soft breezes; or the special relationships with its people. But for everyone there's one vision that can never be forgotten. . . .

For a few weeks each year when the howl of winter's bitter winds subsides, spring comes to the northern steppe. The dust settles. The horizon clears. The rivers overflow with lifegiving waters. Against a carpet of green, the tulips unfold their waxy petals, their tiny seeds staining the mountain streams a ruby red. Poppies, lilies, hyacinths, and roses lift their pure faces to the crystal clear sky. "It's so unsophisticated, so untouched, this marvel of nature," Aman told me.

As swiftly as it arrives, spring's outpouring of green fades into the ocher of summer's intense dust and heat. Through summer, autumn, and winter, the struggle for survival grows harsher. But as surely as day becomes night, spring's beauty returns.

There is something revealing in this victory of life over the steppe's severe obstacles. In it, I believe, the people of this troubled land today can find the strength and hope they need to endure.

Over snow-dappled ground, an aging cameleer guides his beast to the outdoor market. The animal's load includes dried buta, *a desert plant burned for fuel.*

Wind-molded foothills of gravel and loess rise south of Tashkurghan, in the shadow of the U.S.S.R. For a

thousand years this Turkistan town prospered at the crossroads of the east-west caravan trade.   51

Hostel for camels and donkeys, a caravansary offers rest, food, and water. These structures arose as stopping places for caravans; weary travelers lodge in rooms rimming the central courtyard. Here, one man holds a fragrant rose in his teeth. With a basket at his side, the caravansary keeper Jumakhan—a longtime friend of the photographers— gathers dung to sell for fuel and fertilizer. Animals with workaday loads come with their masters across an ancient footbridge (above) leading to Tashkurghan's principal street. Muddy but precious, the River Kholm winds through the town, then on to enrich gardens. On a hilltop to the left stands a crumbling citadel, the Bala Hissar, where the sounds of partridge fighting echo at dawn on Tuesdays and Fridays.

OVERLEAF: Turbaned spectators cheer on their favorite partridge as owners— holding handcrafted wicker cages— monitor the fight. The highly prized birds will battle until one appears the victor, but not to the death.

53

At the close of the morning's business, merchants relax on a wooden platform outside a teahouse. Afghan men spend hours in these establishments—typical of Central Asia—smoking water pipes and discussing business and politics. Deft with feet as well as hands, craftsmen on narrow bazaar streets practice their timeless arts. A wood turner (above), an apprentice at his side, finishes a bedpost with a bowstring lathe. Using thin metal strips and a glue of lime and egg, a patragar, or china mender, repairs porcelain teapots and glass bottles. Scarcity of goods, and habits of thrift, have sustained this craft.

57

*Away from the serene covered bazaar, the noisy outdoor animal market draws farmers
weekly from outlying hamlets to buy, sell, or trade firewood, bushes, and beasts
of burden. This lively event also brings a welcome opportunity for social exchanges.*

Solitary veiled figure hurries past rolling hills and high mud walls on the outskirts of Tashkurghan. Pale in autumn's late afternoon sun, dust-covered peaks (below) surround this fertile valley set amid the barren, sepia steppe. Thick deposits of loess, a fine, powdery soil frequent in this area, have enriched these soils. Farther west near the famed city of Balkh, passengers in a two-wheeled gadi, or horsecart, ride past men harvesting cotton, one of the few crops farmers can sell for a cash income. The ancient practice of irrigation eases the struggle for survival, turning dry, unproductive land into fields of corn, wheat, barley, and luscious melons.

Resplendent 15th-century shrine honoring Ali, son-in-law of the Prophet, dominates the city of Mazar-e-Sharif. Largest mosque in the north, it attracts thousands of devout Muslims yearly in a country where Islam has long governed the lives of all. Legend says pigeons turn white within forty days in this sacred place.

OVERLEAF: *Fierce horsemen,* buz kashi *players gallop wildly across the open steppe in a swirling tempest of dust. The rider on the lead white steed carries the "ball"—the stuffed carcass of a calf—under his thigh toward a distant post while the other players attempt to snatch it from him in this grueling, four-hour game.*

63

Winter dust storm veils a setting sun
as a shepherd and his flock head
toward home across the flat steppe
near the village of Dowlatabad. On
such salt-tinged and ungiving lands,
little wildlife can survive. Bound for
market, a caravan (below) transports
bales of cotton through the snowy,
bitter-cold plains northeast of
Tashkurghan. Though fewer in number
and forced to compete with more
efficient lorries in commerce, caravans
still plod rhythmically across
this legendary land.

Tierra del Fuego

By Leslie Allen
Photographs by Sam Abell

If the cracked parchment ever held a message, time had erased it completely. Discolored and brittle, it lay rumpled on a small table in the captain's quarters of the *Piloto Pardo,* a Chilean naval transport vessel. Scattered around it were other objects, weathered and corroded. An hour ago, they still lay among the rocks where the explorers had stood 152 years earlier. Now the relics were before me—the past come to life.

In 1829, on her first South American voyage, the British ship *Beagle* had sailed through these same desolate channels at the continent's southern tip, in the archipelago known as Tierra del Fuego. As winter approached, six men left her to survey the area in a small schooner. On one of many empty, cliff-bound islands, they had to wait several days for the weather to clear. While they waited, they composed a record of their presence there, signing to it their names and the words "God Save the King." Finally, two of them climbed to the summit of the island, carrying the document in a stoneware bottle which in turn was enclosed in a strong case.

At the top, they looked out over three channels cutting narrow swaths between the broken coasts. Beyond the islands to the south and west stretched the unbroken expanse of the South Pacific Ocean—the ends of the earth. The men placed the case among the rocks, with some coins and other mementos. Then they began their descent. The island was named Skyring for the young lieutenant who scaled its peak.

The account of this is buried deep within the journals of the *Beagle's* first voyage. "I learned of it a few months ago," the *Piloto Pardo's* captain, Eduardo Barison, told me. "I knew that on this trip my ship would pass Skyring Island in daylight, so I decided to send our helicopters out to search for the document." Hovering over Mount Skyring, Lt. Eugenio Arellano had spotted something irregular among its massive rockpiles, and returned to the deck of the *Piloto Pardo* with a plastic bag of artifacts.

One by one, I picked them up from the table and examined them. Four were small commemorative medals, bearing the inscription "H.B.M.S. Adventure and Beagle 1828"—the *Adventure* had been senior ship for the voyage. There were coins minted in England, Brazil, Argentina, Italy. Others were corroded beyond legibility. I held a heavy buckle embossed with a crown-and-anchor insigne and the words "Royal Marines." Stoneware shards had clearly been a bottle once.

The parchment looked too fragile to handle. There was no proof that it was the Skyring document, and even less evidence that the Skyring find itself—which would go to a Chilean museum—was complete. But in the

Isles of sunlight illuminate the Mortimer Strait, one of dozens of waterways in Chilean Tierra del Fuego. Indian canoes and European sailing ships once plied these treacherous waters; now, naval vessels and fishing craft pass but rarely.

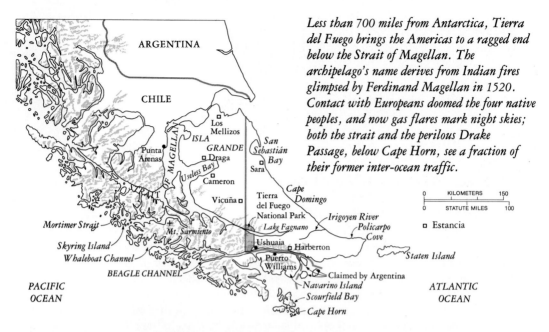

Less than 700 miles from Antarctica, Tierra del Fuego brings the Americas to a ragged end below the Strait of Magellan. The archipelago's name derives from Indian fires glimpsed by Ferdinand Magellan in 1520. Contact with Europeans doomed the four native peoples, and now gas flares mark night skies; both the strait and the perilous Drake Passage, below Cape Horn, see a fraction of their former inter-ocean traffic.

very blankness and mystery of the parchment, there seemed to be a message. Pointing to it, Commander Barison said, "Around here, exploration ashore has been so limited in this century that just by reading the journals of old voyages, we can still make discoveries like this."

Before the 20th century, this remote archipelago was well known to men who made their way here in sailing ships. Some set out to acquire land for their monarchs or find trade routes to the Orient. They learned to expect a harrowing passage, often with delays around Cape Horn. By the 1690s pirates and privateers lurked in the archipelago; later, sea hunters found an abundance of seals and otters. Many came to challenge the unknown in one of the world's most rugged and inhospitable regions. To note even a few of its place-names—Port Famine, Anxious Point, Cape Deceit, Fury Island, Fiasco Bay—is to stand in awe of these people's fortitude.

Ferdinand Magellan was the first, in 1520. The V-shaped, 310-mile-long strait he discovered connects the Atlantic and Pacific Oceans as it severs South America from its southern tip. Below Magellan's strait, the tail of the continent lashes into the Atlantic and then frays into a large and convoluted archipelago amid Pacific breakers. The Indian fires that Magellan glimpsed along the strait's southern shores inspired the Spanish name of Tierra del Fuego, Land of Fire.

Politically as well as geographically, Tierra del Fuego is fragmented. The Denmark-size Isla Grande, "big island," as the 35,000 resident Fuegians call it, is split between Chile and Argentina. Chile controls most of the smaller islands, all but a few uninhabited. But the limits of the narrow Beagle Channel, just south of the big island, account for a complicated, long-standing dispute between the two countries over Argentina's claim to three islands at the channel's mouth. "What's ironic," one Fuegian told me, "is that we're so isolated that we never really became a part of Chile *or* Argentina." Ships of both navies ply these waters, both armies keep troops in the region, and travel across the borders may be restricted.

But during the *Piloto Pardo*'s two-day traverse of the Fuegian channels, I saw only one other craft, a fishing boat with a catch of the region's delectable king crabs. The 20th century seemed far away indeed as I stood on deck, bundled against the wind and cold in five layers of clothing. It was February, and late summer.

Tierra del Fuego's most famous traveler, Charles Darwin—on the *Beagle*'s second voyage, between 1831 and 1836—looked south from the Strait of Magellan and wrote that "the distant channels between the mountains appeared from their gloominess to lead beyond the confines of this world." Now we were in that other, uninhabited world; the low, vibrating hum of the ship's engines, mingling with the sounds of the wind, only emphasized its silence.

We sailed among rutted, rocky islands and half-submerged mountains. Their shadowy peaks rose right out of the water; the mountain valleys, filled with water, were deep sounds and fjords. In some places the aqua tints of huge glaciers met the channels' black waters. Elsewhere, silvery waterfalls cascaded through forested mountain ravines. The twin peaks of Mount Sarmiento, ice sculptures of some 7,500 feet, floated in and out of sight above the clouds that obscured the Darwin Cordillera.

A few hours later, the *Piloto Pardo* anchored briefly in Desolate Bay, on the Whaleboat Channel, and I set out on a short expedition to Burnt Island. Far below me—too far—a small launch bobbed in the water as I scrambled over the ship's railing and gingerly made my way down a swaying rope boarding ladder. Otherwise aptly named, Desolate Bay presented a carnival of bird life. Large, flightless steamer ducks scattered before the launch, churning the water on whirling wings; their common name comes from that splashy propulsion, which reminded me of Mississippi sidewheelers. Slender cormorants flapped black-and-white against the gray sky. Snow-white male kelp geese dotted the rocks off Burnt Island. They appeared to be alone; but drawing closer, I saw that each one stood in quiet monogamy with his deeply camouflaged mate.

The world's southernmost trees are constant visual reminders of the fierce westerlies that rake Tierra del Fuego. Every tree, every grove, it seems, leans eastward. In more protected areas, beeches 40 feet tall thrust sinuous branches out of wildly knotted trunks. But Burnt Island's south shore did not sustain even these tormented specimens. After climbing over a low wall of rock at the water's edge, I found myself walking on treetops—a foot or two off the ground! In this carpet of dwarf beech trees was, I thought, an example of fitness to survive, as exquisite as any that Darwin observed in this unforgiving region.

Mostly, the tiny twisted branches crunched underfoot; occasionally they exposed the mossy ground underneath, making the climb more difficult. I guided myself upward by the sound of a nearby waterfall, and finally stood by the lake that fed it. Its water tasted sweeter than a spring's. And from this lofty vantage point, island after island rose into the distance like an endless sequence of great Pacific swells.

Here and there amidst these islands, the Chilean navy maintains small watchposts. I visited one of them to attend a Mass in a tiny chapel built of unhewn beech logs. Just 12 miles north of Cape Horn, Scourfield Bay at Wollaston Island may be the loneliest place in the world to live. On two-month stints, two men at a time are stationed there.

"The sailors here felt the need for God," said the *Piloto Pardo*'s chaplain as the wind sang through the chapel and an ornate censer swung back and forth. "And so the Stella Maris Chapel was built, and consecrated in 1978." Various naval ships had contributed manpower and supplies; their emblems hung from the little white brick altar.

Ending the rites, the chaplain blew out the flickering flame of the chapel's single candle. As he repacked his vestments in his briefcase, a thin beam of sunlight momentarily framed a painting of the Madonna. But by the time I stepped outside, the sky was overcast again.

It would not be fitting for the sun to shine on Cape Horn, where fog and mist and cloud prevail from day to day. Just to see this last baleful cliff is to feel the legendary darkness that inspired Jules Verne, Edgar Allan Poe, Herman Melville—to imagine the spectral winter radiance that Samuel Taylor Coleridge evoked in "The Rime of the Ancient Mariner." To these writers, Cape Horn was the ultimate land's end.

Geographically, it is only a southern fragment of the Andes Mountains, which veer eastward through Staten Island and continue as a submarine ridge. The archipelago's southernmost outliers are the Diego Ramírez islets, a bleak little group described as "the end beyond the end"; they rise in the Drake Passage, which separates Cape Horn from Antarctica. Francis Drake himself survived the storms of these waters, in 1578. Dutch mariners, Willem Schouten and Jakob Le Maire, assigned the name "Hoorn" in 1616, for Schouten's home community.

In time, east-west sea traffic moved south from the Strait of Magellan to the Drake Passage. That fact speaks only of the strait's incredible treachery—a mortal threat to sailing ships, a menace even to steamers—for the alternate route offers some of the world's most dangerous water. There westerlies deflected off the Andes finally vent their fury. The winds, the currents, the "graybeards" or seas as high as 60 feet, the occasional monster icebergs and the perennial squalls enhanced the yarns of every sailor who lived to tell the tale. Many didn't. Just between 1850 and 1900, some hundreds of ships went down off the Horn.

Newfound artifacts—possibly cached in 1829 by officers of H.M.S. Beagle—come to light on board a Chilean naval ship as Lt. Eugenio Arellano describes his search for them. From the find (opposite): commemorative medals.

Both routes lost importance after the Panama Canal opened in 1914, and "Cape Stiff" loomed unsighted for many a day. In 1945 Chile designated Horn and its neighbor isles Cape Horn National Park, a "virgin reserve." The world's southernmost national park is uninhabited; it remains a defiant monument to men against the sea.

From the air—from a helicopter—Horn Island looks savagely graceful. Its granite slopes rise steeply, clothed in peat and low evergreen thickets. Beyond a dark lake, the cape itself climbs to a peak, then plunges to the water in pinnacled cliffs. The Americas appear to end in a long sliver of rock, mantled in leaping foam, pointing to Antarctica.

For centuries before Europeans discovered it, Horn Island was known to a small tribe of Indians who ranged the waters from the Beagle Channel south in bark canoes. They were the Yamana, generally known as Yahgan, whose ways so appalled the young Darwin that he called them "the most abject and miserable creatures I anywhere beheld." Practically naked, they moved their campsites from inlet to inlet, feeding on shellfish, seals, and birds. Not until the late 19th century did missionaries working among them begin to discover their complex language and rich spiritual lives. By then, the Yahgan were well on their way to extinction. A people hardy enough to survive for thousands of years in such an inhospitable climate was felled by measles and other diseases brought by Europeans.

They are gone now, except for a living link in the person of one childless widow. Ironically, her nickname is Abuela Rosa: Grandma Rosa. I visited Abuela Rosa at her home in Ukika, a cluster of little blue-and-yellow houses down the road from the town of Puerto Williams on Navarino Island. Her neighbors peeked through their windows, their dogs barking at my approach. The view from her doorway was a framed picture postcard: the north shore of Navarino Island, a small white fishing boat in the ribbon-flat Beagle Channel, the snowcapped mountains of the big island just two miles across the channel. Stooped to a little more than four feet in her flower-patterned housedress, Rosa turned and walked slowly to her chair.

"The children here make fun of me because I can't read," she said in fluent Spanish, picking up flattened reeds to weave into a small basket. "But I have eyes to learn." She pointed to the centerpiece of her two-room house: a large television set. Three cats pawed mussel shells on the floor; the smells of raw wool and boiled lamb ripened in the closeness of her kitchen. I asked about her childhood.

"I don't know my age, but I was already a woman when my friends were born, and my friends are old now. I traveled in a canoe, and I ate seals and birds." Her creased face opened into a toothless smile. "I still do when I can. The white men's food was bad for us, especially sugar."

Her eyes lost their faraway look. "Now, there are sheep and people. The government gives me money. I like church, but my friends won't let me go because it's so far away."

When I started to leave, Abuela Rosa remarked, "I used to speak English, you know." I asked her how her Yahgan was. Her answer was a song, soft and melodious—about work, she said afterward. She sang the Yahgan song for a long time. Then, by way of farewell: "Dream of me tonight."

Besides Abuela Rosa, the Yahgan have a monument on Navarino Island in the form of Puerto Williams's small, excellent museum. Its director, Oscar Gálvez, had been studying them during the last four years.

"They were the most isolated of Tierra del Fuego's four tribes," he explained. "Since they had so little opportunity for exchange with other peoples, they didn't evolve culturally. When the Europeans settled here, the Yahgan went straight from the Stone Age to the modern age.

"There has been very little archaeological work here, and we need it. As the town grows, construction destroys the Yahgan middens, the shell piles—and everyone wants to take home an arrowhead as a souvenir."

Oscar Gálvez lettered a sign for a new exhibit, and our talk turned to Puerto Williams itself. This cheerful community of 1,200, largely naval personnel, claims the title of world's southernmost town.

"But we have none of the usual small-town idiosyncrasies," Oscar said. "Most people here are from big cities, and they bring their needs and customs with them. We started our own television and FM radio stations.

What other town this size can say that? We're getting our own ski area." The roads, he told me, will remain unpaved, to keep life simple. "And for real tranquillity," he added, deadpan, "we have a terrible phone system."

If anything epitomizes Puerto Williams's isolation, it is the one balky radio telephone that connects the town to the outside world. All conversations are public, for the tiny room with the phone also functions as post office and general meeting place. Garish government posters adorn its walls; a bulletin board displays telegrams and two typed lists: "Correspondence received for gentlemen" and "Correspondence received for ladies." As I entered one day, I was greeted by a burst of high-pitched static. The operator nonchalantly pronounced the circuit "completely dead," but most of the assemblage remained, faithfully awaiting the next resuscitation.

Puerto Williams's other link to the world, air service, also receives much attention. Residents know the schedules by heart. "Most people have flown in so many times," I was told, "that they go up to the cockpit and offer landing suggestions." When I left a few days later, people stood on the airstrip waving white handkerchiefs. The woman seated next to me waved back, then turned to me and said, "That's the Tuesday diversion."

Tierra del Fuego is still a land of pioneers. Most lead lives of isolation and toil, gaining a spiritual independence that makes their homeland seem as much a state of mind as a place. On Isla Grande, there are physical resemblances to the old American West. Arid grasslands—a last remnant of the Patagonian steppe—roll south from the Strait of Magellan, becoming moist and green, then gradually rising to forested hillsides and beyond to a crown of mountains. And beyond: water.

Man-made landmarks suggest similarities, too. Oil rigs bristle in the strait and along its southern shore. Farther south, abandoned dredges tell of another, short-lived boom, a turn-of-the-century gold rush. Instead of roads, the barbed wire of sheep pastures speeds to the horizon, or encloses a few old headstones in the middle of a windswept plain. One of them reads: "Erected by his fellow employees in memory of John Saldine, who was killed by Indians on 20th July 1898." Those Indians, warriors of the Ona tribe, are gone, like the Yahgan; but lonely shepherds and sawyers still fill the small-town dives on weekend nights.

And in the hills, I met a wizened old miner living alone in a mud-roofed hut. He served cognac in plastic cups and told me he couldn't remember how many times he'd been married. He complained about the falling price of gold, then took me outside in the sleet to show me how he panned the gravel in a maze of little channels.

On the big island, I had the feeling that I was traveling back in time. Perhaps it was because Tierra del Fuego is still a frontier, which most of us no longer have.

"It is land's end, the *ne plus ultra*—no more beyond. Only Antarctica is more distant and difficult than Tierra del Fuego," said Mateo Martinić, a man whose passion for this land has been a life's work. The son of Croatian immigrants, he is a former governor of the province of Magallanes, which includes Chilean Tierra del Fuego, and the author of numerous books and articles on the region. Now he directs the Instituto de la Patagonia, a multidisciplinary research center in Punta Arenas, Chile, across the Strait of Magellan from the big island.

"The permanent presence of man here, starting more than ten

thousand years ago, is a miracle," he exclaimed. "Everything is difficult: the climate, the geography, the isolation." Until the arrival of commercial air service in 1946, a boat trip to the next port up the Chilean coast took eight to ten days; there were no roads. "The isolation is especially important because it caused the autonomous development of a society.

"In some ways what we have here resembles what happened in the United States and Canada because of the mixture of ethnic groups," he pointed out. "And what a man was worth depended on his own effort and intelligence, and not on what he owned." We talked about the different folk who settled here: the Scots and the English who came to raise sheep; the miners and laborers from what is now Yugoslavia; the Chileans and Argentines colonizing their own south; the Spaniards, Germans, French, and others.

They have melted into a landscape of sheep ranches and oil camps and a handful of towns. Tierra del Fuego, Mateo Martinić believes, "will always be an empty land."

When Ana Hansen Brstilo stepped onto the gale-swept shores of Useless Bay in 1916, it was, relatively, much emptier. She was 14, born in Punta Arenas of a Danish father and a mother from Alsace. They had sent her over to the big island to help a bachelor uncle work a few rented acres and to care for aged grandparents. Sixty-five years later, she welcomed me to Estancia Draga. In Spanish *estancia* means spread or ranch, and *draga* is a Serbo-Croatian word for beloved. Of all Tierra del Fuego's eloquent names, it seemed the most appropriate.

Outside, a young pet guanaco stood impassively as the wind shrieked off Useless Bay at 50 knots. Inside, the house filled with the aroma of creampuffs baking in the woodburning stove, and an open fire crackled on the hearth. Entranced by the oddity of visitors, Ana's little granddaughter Paola scampered about happily.

"When I was a girl here," Ana said, "I didn't know anything about friends and outings. My grandmother and I were the only women around. The only fun I had was panning for gold once in a while.

"When my grandmother died, the vigil lasted five days because there was no way to take her to town for the funeral. At two o'clock one morning, a cutter sailed into Useless Bay. My uncle ran down to the beach and built a fire. The boat stopped to help us." Ana paused.

"It turned out that my grandparents had come over on that same cutter. Their trip had been so rough that my grandmother told the captain she'd never set foot on his boat again. The captain told her that he would see her again—and he did."

At Estancia Draga, Paola Brstilo, age 4, feeds a young guanaco, an orphan and pet. Docility wanes as guanacos, undomesticated members of the camel family, grow older; 13,000 roam wild on the big island.

Ana married the young man from Dalmatia who rented the land where Estancia Draga now stands, and change came to be measured in the births of her five sons. She rode into town on horseback the day before the eldest was born. The trip took all day. The next year, the journey was made by ox cart; then came a borrowed Model T. When the fifth little boy was born, a midwife came out to the estancia—arriving three hours after the birth. Her husband left her for life in town; Ana reared the boys and ran the farm alone. Little by little she bought the rented acres, as her sons grew old enough to help her. And now: 5,500 sheep on 6,916 acres—a small estancia by local standards, but free and clear.

"Before," Ana said, "people came to visit in ox carts and there were no roads. Now there are roads but so many friends are gone."

The end of the rock-strewn road on the Chilean side of the island is about 70 miles southeast of Estancia Draga. It passes shallow lakes filled with black-necked swans, shepherds roasting lambs in a driving rain, still-life groupings of wild guanaco—and then halts in the formidable shadow of the Darwin Cordillera. But to the east, on the Argentine side of the border, the mountains become lower and gentler; a dirt road winds upward between their glaciated faces and then descends to the Beagle Channel and the town of Ushuaia, Tierra del Fuego's oldest settlement.

In 1871, the Reverend Thomas Bridges, an Englishman, and his family became the island's first permanent white residents when they came to serve an Anglican mission here. Later, Ushuaia became the site of a maximum-security prison and a town grew up around it. The prison now holds naval stores, and Ushuaia, in its latest incarnation, has become Tierra del Fuego's tourist stop. The town of 11,000 boasts first-class hotels and good restaurants, chic shops and tango nights. Commercial flights whine overhead; sailboats and occasional cruise ships gleam in the pretty harbor. In summertime, visitors from Buenos Aires crowd the narrow streets, toting low-duty purchases in shopping bags that say "Tierra del Fuego."

Ushuaia also has a 360-degree view of snowcapped mountains and a 154,000-acre national park next door. On clear, calm days, a lovelier setting is hard to imagine, as the sunlit peaks form a broken white border between a porcelain sky and the sapphire of the Beagle Channel.

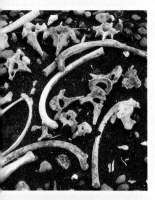

The weather changed rapidly the day I explored Tierra del Fuego National Park, and the abatement of each squall was marked by rainbows arcing through the mist. With me was wildlife biologist Walter Sielfeld, of the Instituto de la Patagonia. As we drove toward Lapataia Bay, white spots seemed to dance before my eyes. Rabbit tails. Hundreds of them.

"They were introduced from Europe, for domestic purposes," Walter said, "and, of course, some escaped. They had no natural enemies here, and became a pest because they competed with sheep for graze."

Within a luxuriant stand of beech and Winter's bark trees, I forgot I was less than 700 miles from Antarctica. Ferns covered the ground, dotted with the tiny crimson fruit of the devil's strawberry plant. Here, green austral parakeets flit among branches; and in summer, orchids bloom in shades of yellow and green. But beyond the forest, and beyond a clearing littered with timber, were the ruddy sphagnum bogs of the moorland. Giant green pincushions—the balsam bog plant—filled the air with their resinous odor. The mossy ground squished wetter and wetter around our boots, and we found ourselves at a pond dammed by beavers: yet another animal brought from abroad and now considered a pest.

I saw small hawks rising from the trees; three larger hawks wheeled as if in formation above Lapataia Bay. I had not even hoped to see an Andean condor, the giant carrion-eater that soars on a wingspan of ten feet or more. Yet one appeared, imposing even at a distance, poised upon air. For as long as I could see it circling—about two minutes—it did not move its black wings. Then it vanished among the distant peaks.

If Tierra del Fuego's skies are home to the world's largest soaring birds, the condor and the albatross, its waters hold a rich variety of the greatest mammals, whales. Fifteen kinds, including the endangered baleen whales, roam offshore or make seasonal migrations. Another eleven species of porpoises and dolphins—and possibly more—play in these waters. But research has been scant because the area is so inaccessible.

Strandings are frequent. One of the most dramatic occurred in 1979, when 126 pilot whales beached themselves on Navarino Island. "Through strandings," Walter told me, "we've been able to gather some important details about species that are practically unknown."

In varying states of completeness, skeletons of porpoises and dolphins fill the cabinets and line the shelves, countertops, and ceiling beams of Natalie Goodall's home in Ushuaia. "I'm sort of an old-style naturalist, a natural-born collector," Natalie said. She showed me the skull of a Commerson's dolphin, rare beyond these waters. "I just pick up everything that comes along."

As a young, Ohio-born schoolteacher, she had become fascinated with Tierra del Fuego; she paid a visit in 1962. She met Thomas Bridges's great-grandson, Tom Goodall, and a year later returned as his bride to Harberton, the Bridges estancia on the Beagle Channel.

"Once, walking the beaches, I found a couple of dolphin skulls. I showed them to a visiting expert who said, 'I've never held one of these before!' It's much more fun when everyone oohs and aahs." Now she divides her time among Ushuaia, Harberton, and the island's lonely beaches. Her collection—the best anywhere for the sea mammals of this region—includes the bones of more than 900 whales, porpoises, and dolphins.

On a bright, raw morning I arrived by launch at Harberton, and was immediately reminded of her. Two slender bones—from a whale's jaw—arched and met over the front gate. And later, in the bathroom, I saw a towel holder fashioned of . . . a whale's vertebral disk.

Harberton, dating from 1886, is Argentine Tierra del Fuego's oldest estancia, and one of the most isolated. The family airplane is a key means of transportation.

"From natives in skin robes to finding you can fly is a very big change indeed," said Bridges's granddaughter Clarita Goodall, herself a grandmother. She was showing me glass cases filled with Indian hunting tools, bird-bone needles, and shell necklaces. "Father had these things especially made when he realized the Indians were disappearing."

Her uncle, Lucas Bridges, had been the first white person to befriend the guanaco-hunting Ona Indians of the inland. His memoir, *Uttermost Part of the Earth,* remains the preeminent work on Tierra del Fuego.

I looked at Clarita's own patient, delicate watercolors of Fuegian flowers. "You must have an interest to be happy here," she said in her English accent, and it was clearly a family theme. "We have plenty of dull days with gray skies. Other people might not like to get their noses cold."

Clarita's American daughter-in-law, Natalie, takes a special interest in

At San Sebastián Bay, beachcomber Karin Laubscher displays a sperm whale's tooth to Natalie Goodall. Metallic sulfides in the bay-floor mud have blackened a whale's jawbone. The bay's shallows often trap sea mammals. Opposite: Bones of sea lions litter dark sands; lichens yellow a half-buried skull.

shipwrecks. "There are hundreds not far from here," she told me. In the Strait of Magellan, I had already seen the magnificent fragments of the *Olympian,* an old iron side-wheeler; her two rusted paddles, 32 feet in diameter, lay intact on the beach.

Now we were flying east above the Beagle Channel, looking for other wrecks. Below us, long streamers of kelp waved languidly just below the water's surface. Then the bow of the *Sarmiento,* an Argentine cargo steamer, emerged from the water. Seemingly in supplication, the curving lines of her prow converged and pointed skyward.

"A lot of ships went around the Horn at the time of the California gold rush," Natalie said. "Some carried coal, which frequently caught on fire. Others were lost because of poor navigation." Capricious weather and inadequate instruments made every season dangerous—and still do.

When we rounded the easternmost tip of the big island, the mountains lining the Beagle Channel had given way to curving inlets backed by boggy wetlands and fronted by long tidal flats. It was the most desolate vista yet. We saw only one wreck, the three-masted *Duchess of Albany,* on her side in the sand. Many other ships had met their end near here, but they lay in the depths. Below us, there were no signs of life, just reminders of it.

The six stranded whales reminded me of shipwrecks. They were covered with sand and decaying on the shores of San Sebastián Bay, on the northeastern part of Isla Grande. This area is as flat as the Beagle Channel zone is mountainous, and the bay is a great shallow trap for marine mammals. Like seashells, the bones of sea lions were scattered about in the dark sand.

It was my last day in Tierra del Fuego, and I was driving north along the Atlantic coast. All day long, the sea was a vast, deep-blue backdrop: to sheepskins drying on the fences of huge estancias; to the fields of sheep; to the beached whales; to the headstones of Scottish immigrants—to the history of Tierra del Fuego itself.

The 20th century was at hand, too. That night as I drove back along the coast, the sky glowed orange with the reflection of gas flares and the promise of oil, not with the Indian fires that inspired a name.

In the darkness, I passed the old mission of the Salesian Fathers. They had come at the end of the 19th century because in Italy their founder, St. John Bosco, had dreamed of this "wild region." His dreams were of savage warriors, and of riches lying undiscovered in the ground.

I thought of someone else's dream. Six weeks earlier, as I was arriving in this part of the world, a young man had stood in the lingering dusk at the edge of Punta Arenas. He strapped himself into a hang glider and tried to fly to the big island, 18 miles across the Strait of Magellan.

He never made it. Most people said he was crazy to try, and, at the time, I was inclined to agree. But now I thought otherwise: Dacron wings seemed little more fragile than the sailing ships had been when they came to this archipelago in their time. Now I thought that the young man was simply one more for whom the raw challenge of Tierra del Fuego was an implacable lure—and a dream.

Living link to a lost people, Rosa Miličić of Navarino Island recalls her Yahgan girlhood. Her memories and knowledge of the Indian tongue draw visitors, who often leave with a Yahgan-style basket; an example of her handiwork hangs behind her.

A *"noble and even sublime spectacle" to Charles Darwin, a mariners' landmark for centuries, Mount Sarmiento (above) culminates in glistening twin spires high above lesser outliers of the Darwin Cordillera. Honoring the English naturalist, who saw them in 1833, the partly submerged mountains—Tierra del Fuego's grandest—rise to summits exceeding 7,500 feet. Below, daybreak light catches glacier-streaked slopes along the Beagle Channel. Darwin likened the immense glaciers he saw to "great frozen Niagaras": Marinelli, the longest (left), paves 12 miles of the Darwin Range. The high peaks that shadow it shed frost-loosened rocks which form lateral and medial moraines, dark stripes on the rumpled ice.*

Pristine setting of Navarino Island lends charm to Puerto Williams, on the Beagle Channel. Permanently moored at the town's western edge, the Micalvi *transported supplies that built Puerto Williams as a Chilean naval base in 1953. The town of 1,200 now claims the title of world's southernmost. Bad weather often closes the airfield, and border disputes with Argentina, just across the channel, accent the isolation—but gentle hillsides and Navarino's snaggled Teeth, Los Dientes, offer superb recreation.*

OVERLEAF: *Less than 80 miles to the south stands Cape Horn. Here, the author says, "the Americas appear to end in a long sliver of rock, mantled in leaping foam, pointing to Antarctica."*

Sheep ranches called estancias *spread over northern grasslands, giving Tierra del Fuego its classic products: wool and mutton. Near the Strait of Magellan, in Chile, a bull's skull marks the entrance to Estancia Los Mellizos—The Twins. On a day of wind speeds passing 50 knots, a shepherd prepares dinner, roast lamb, at Estancia Cameron. Starting in the 1940s, the Chilean government broke the island's massive corporate holdings into smaller units; with 53,000 sheep, 1,350 cattle, 240,000 acres, and 23 owners, Cameron remains the last great venture of its kind.*

Between showers, a wispy rainbow tints the sky over Estancia Vicuña, one of the southernmost ranches on the Chilean side of the big island. Increased elevation and rainfall in this area account for wide swatches of green in meadows interrupted by beech trees and bogs—and occasional police outposts. Forested hillsides hold only a few isolated sawmills. Left uninhabited by an absentee owner, Vicuña's once-elegant "big house" still offers an impressive eastward view from fanciful turrets and unshuttered windows. Next door, Lulu, a caretaker's pet, inspects a young visitor from nearby Pampa Guanaco—Plain of the Guanaco.

OVERLEAF: *Afternoon reflections mottle Lake Fagnano, beyond flowers of the exotic herb* Achillea millefolium. *Known for its wind-whipped turbulence, the 62-mile-long lake, Tierra del Fuego's largest, stretches through Argentine mountains and parkland, its waters flowing west into Chile. In 1949, an earthquake lowered surrounding lands and joined neighboring lakes to Fagnano; a fault line comparable to California's San Andreas zone underlies the flooded terrain.*

Red-roofed buildings of Harberton—Argentine Tierra del Fuego's first estancia—face northeast across a Beagle Channel inlet. Yahgan Indians led missionary Thomas Bridges to this spot, and in 1886 the government ceded him land for the ranch, named for his wife's native Devonshire village. Today, a great-grandson manages the 50,000 acres of pasture, forest, mountains, and water. In the garden, flowering Sweet William dwarfs a watchful farm cat.

Rendered in the delicate palette of Clarita Bridges Goodall, a yellow violet (right) blooms on paper. "I started painting Fuegian plants in 1923, when it seemed that some species were disappearing because the sheep trampled them," says the artist, at home at Harberton. Her precise watercolors number more than 100. She gathers inspiration roaming the big island, where, in surprising variety, small plants and shrubs add color to a harsh land. From left, below: Crimson rainberries ripen in summer on forest clearings; an orchid, Gavilea australis, blooms elegantly amid spiny bushes; flowers of the holly-leafed barberry, a shrub, appear in profusion as winter ends; thirsty Ourisia ruelloides thrives near remote waterfalls and on riverbanks, its bell-like blossoms appearing in November.

THOMAS D. GOODALL (ABOVE, RIGHT, AND FAR RIGHT)

Beech woods hinting of autumn and peat bogs beyond share ruddy hues along the
Irigoyen River's course to the Atlantic Ocean. Of the calafate's fruit (left), Fuegians
say, "Taste it once and you'll return to Tierra del Fuego."

*Home on the pampa:
Sturdy crossbreeds of
Estancia Sara—the big
island's largest—head
across the treeless flat
expanse of northeastern
Tierra del Fuego.
At right, a shepherd's
balky horse resists
saddling outside a barn
weatherproofed, in
Fuegian fashion, with
sheets of corrugated metal.
Day's work done, manager
Alejandro (Sandy) Mann
relaxes in an easy
chair of solid comfort.*

Staunch in his saddle despite a chilling rain, a hand at Estancia Sara herds sheep to the sorting pens—some to the slaughterhouse; weary sheep dog Tango flops down, panting, to rest. Such drives occur, after shearing and dipping, in late summer and fall—that is, late February to May. At big estancias a drive may take several days; the area offers such thin grazing that on average one sheep requires three acres. On Isla Grande, however, sheep outnumber the 35,000 people by 50 to 1. These Corriedales produce prized wool, worthy of the breed's Merino ancestry, but today stockmen complain of falling prices brought on by competition from synthetic fibers. They also contend with problems of transportation. Some must hire a barge to get the fleece to a buyer. In the past, ships of the Chilean and Argentine navies often carried wool for remote estancias; but this practice has become less common since the early 1950s as graded—but unpaved—roads have appeared.

Atlantic waters wash the iron hull of the British Duchess of Albany, *wrecked in 1893 near Policarpo Cove—*

on a coast notorious as a graveyard for Horn-bound ships of many flags.

Ensconced in mist, Cape Domingo juts prow-like into the Atlantic. Atop the sheer-sided headland a light

beams warning; far below, waves break on kelp-strewn flats.

The Santa Martas

By James Billipp
Photographs by the Author

Late in the second day of our descent from base camp at 15,000 feet, the six men of the 1974 Moby Honcho Andean Expedition emerged from a canopy of avocado trees and stumbled to a halt on the rocky bank of the Río Donachui. The Indian village of Sogrome, where we planned to camp, lay across the river and beyond the next hill.

"I've had it!" bellowed our 24-year-old leader, Bill McKinney. "I'm too old to be humping this kind of weight around, freezing my tail off and risking my neck." Buddies from college days, the rest of us just grinned at him and he went on melodramatically: "No more expedition climbing for *this* honcho. After the Santa Martas, Everest would only bore me anyhow."

Known to mountaineers as the world's highest coastal range, the Sierra Nevada de Santa Marta is a vertical wilderness rising abruptly to snow peaks within 30 miles of the palm-lined Caribbean coast. With its Siamese twin, Pico Cristóbal Colón, Pico Simón Bolívar shares the honor of being Colombia's tallest mountain. Of virtually equal height—nearly 19,000 feet—both "the Discoverer" and "the Liberator" offer superb mixed climbing; we had come for the adventure of it, risks and all. Only a few days earlier Bill had experienced a close call on the east face of Pico Bolívar.

While the rest of us waited at base camp, he was on a new route with David Kallgren, a mountaineering instructor from Wyoming. The best rock-climber among us, Bill was leading the most difficult section. As David belayed him from a ledge below, Bill worked his way up a narrow crack in the granite wall, jamming his fingers and the tips of his rock-shoes in the fissure. The crack was full of muck and surprises. Every ten or fifteen feet he placed a chock, and clipped the rope to it.

He was inching up the edge of a huge granite slab when a sudden *crrrack* rang out and the slab peeled away from the wall, flashing down past David's face. An instant later Bill was dangling upside down in the air near David, stunned, his head only six inches above the belay ledge. Beneath the ledge the east face dropped away to the glacier, hundreds of feet below.

David had watched in horror as the top chock pulled loose. Luckily, the others held. Bill was bruised and shaken, but otherwise OK. They decided to push on; but because the critical handhold had fallen, they prudently altered their route, following an icy ledge.

We at base camp knew nothing of this. Bob Harris, Jim Wells, John Bollard, and I lazed about all day, reading paperbacks and sunbathing. At dusk, our binoculars revealed two black dots just below the summit, silhouetted by a fiery sunset. "All right!" we yelled. "The east face *direct!*"

Palms and peaks share Colombia's northern coast, where snows of the Sierra Nevada de Santa Marta loom above seaside terrain of tropical luxuriance. The massif —highest of the world's coastal ranges—rises from the shores of the Caribbean.

With peaks of 19,000 feet, the sierra covers 5,000 square miles. To the east lie the Andes, and Venezuela. Ridges trending east-west make for dramatic shifts in climate and for difficult travel, helping to keep the region secluded. Officially declared a reserve, it has remained virtually untainted, if not untouched.

The sky faded, and our mood sobered. Why had it taken them so long? How would they negotiate the descent of that knife-edge ridge in the dark? They had a pocket flashlight, but would the battery hold out?

We delayed supper as long as we could. Around midnight we decided to try to sleep. We might need all our strength for a search. . . .

In fact the descent, says David, was "perhaps even more memorable." A bivouac seemed even riskier than finding their way down before moon-rise, with a strong wind whipping up billows of snow. Below the Colón glacier they groped about looking for the high camp. A glistening dimness might be a wet slab of rock, or a frozen pond; and the shift of one rock underfoot hurled David into deep water. Luckily, they found the camp in time to save him from freezing. Next day, sweating in the hot glare of the sun, they walked five hours to base camp. A success, but not an easy one.

A week later, crossing the Río Donachui at Sogrome, Bill was still drained from that climb. Shouting over the water's roar, he announced his next ideal trip. "Next winter, I'm going someplace civilized, like Yosemite. You can sleep late, take a bus to the foot of the climb, and be back sippin' cold beer in a warm bar by sundown!" He adjusted the shoulder straps of his mammoth pack and started across a bridge of huge tree trunks. "What are *you* doing next winter?" he yelled.

Pausing on the bridge, I gazed down into the clear racing waters. Next year? In the rippling translucence below I seemed to recognize each of the streams, lakes, and glaciers we had passed upstream. Someday, I resolved, I would return to these mountains. Maybe not next year, but someday. Accounts of earlier expeditions described the area in superlatives. Its attractions, we had found, were not exaggerated.

Thomas D. Cabot's 1939 expedition scaled Pico Colón and produced the first accurate maps of the southeast slopes of the Santa Martas. "By almost any definition," Cabot wrote, "they form the world's highest coastal range and one of the highest ranges from base to summit. Add to this the wild Indians, the ancient lost civilization, the tremendous variety of flora and fauna, the superb granitic cliffs, large glaciers and crystal streams, the ideal camping conditions on the high paramos in our winter, and it becomes amazing that alpinists have neglected this range for so long."

Cabot himself told me one drawback to climbing here: the reluctance of local Indians to let foreigners—including Colombians—into their sacred mountains. More and more climbers came. Often they reported difficulty with the Indians, and some were turned back. More recently, the cultivation of marijuana by smugglers in the foothills, along with looting at archaeological sites, further estranged the Indians.

We entered Sogrome unchallenged and found it deserted. The mule bags containing some of our gear lay where we had camped five weeks before, but neither our rented mules nor our Indian mule driver, Atilio Villafaña, could be seen. We flopped to the ground exhausted, and disconcerted. We had counted on paying or bartering for food here; where had the people gone?

At nightfall we dropped our last bouillon cubes into a pot of boiling water, downed this meager fare, and turned in, assuring each other that Atilio would come for us with his mules in the morning.

With the stars overhead and the snoring all around, I found it impossible to sleep. I got out my headlamp and journal, and reviewed our trip.

We had gotten in by sheer luck. The Ica Indians at the village of Donachui refused to let us pass. John Bollard recalled a newspaper report that a partial solar eclipse was due the following day; I decided to tell the Ica—in Spanish—to expect it. A group of stern young men gathered about our camp. But that evening an exhibition of advanced play with a glow-in-the-dark Frisbee finally brought smiles to their impassive faces. After the eclipse, some of them brought a message from the *mamo,* or shaman-priest, of Sogrome, the next village uphill. Apparently Ica astronomy did not run to such predictions; the priest was impressed by our knowledge. He would let us visit their sacred snows, provided that we rented our mules from his kinsmen and hired two of them as guides.

We had climbed six major peaks, and enjoyed our days at base camp. We had met some diplomats from Bogotá, on vacation, who were climbing El Guardián, the most strikingly beautiful peak. They disappeared on the summit in a sudden snowstorm, and we staged an arduous three-day search. Their bodies were located, we learned, in a hot shower at a hotel in Valledupar—they had made their way out to the south, through the Ica village of San Sebastián.

Early the next morning, Atilio showed up. Most apologetically, he told us that he wouldn't be able to travel for a few days. His sister-in-law Rosina had been bitten by a dog, and was expected to die. Her funeral would require the presence of all Villafañas in the area.

Thinking of our medical kit, I offered the expedition's help. Atilio accepted gratefully, but warned that his uncle would not want a group of foreigners at the healing ceremonies. I spoke fluent Spanish, so I took our copy of *Medicine for Mountaineering* and followed Atilio into the hills.

As we went through a patch of vividly green coca bushes I heard voices. The trail opened onto a circular patio of land leveled from the hillside. Some 30 or 40 Indians—the people of Sogrome—clustered about a large house, and I felt their eyes on me as I followed Atilio to the group's center. There Atilio's uncle, the mamo Juan Bautista, sat beside his patient, who reclined in a hammock. He smiled a welcome around the wad of coca leaves swelling his cheek. He said little, though his Spanish was good.

Rosina Villafaña was indeed very ill, one leg horribly swollen with infection, her pain obvious despite her stoic silence. At least, I thought, she did not have rabies; I brought out the brightly colored pills, antibiotics and pain-killers, warning that they might not work—it might be too late.

Mamo Juan Bautista took them eagerly and performed a complicated rite over them, evidently to cleanse them of foreign contamination. I gave him a day's supply and left with a gift of oranges, plantains, and fresh eggs.

When I went back with more medicine, I watched Juan Bautista's treatments with growing interest. To fill one of his esoteric prescriptions, we carried Rosina in her hammock, slung from a long pole, on a roundabout trip to the Río Donachui. Here the mamo directed his sister to fish dead insects from a stagnant pool. Later he may have fed them to the patient. I chatted with him, and he asked how we had predicted the eclipse. We had read about it in a newspaper, I said. He responded with a long "ahhhh," nodding gravely.

Spring-fed waterfall dashes onto roadside boulders at Minca, in the coastal forest. Each year two long rainy seasons wash out the inland roads, trails, and paths.

I grew fascinated by the Ica; it thrilled me to be among them. I was reluctant to leave when, after three days on antibiotics, Rosina felt much better and Atilio was free to guide us out of the sierra.

We passed our Frisbee field at Donachui in the morning and by late afternoon reached Atanquez, on the fringe of what the Indians call "civilización." Atilio, by now our good friend, would not sit at dinner with us in the tiny hotel, but ate from a plate in the street. He was not at ease here; beds, hotels, and money pertained to our world. At our parting Atilio encouraged me to come climbing again. With a laugh that challenged me to prove him wrong, he predicted that I would never return.

During the following months the Moby Honcho Expedition traveled south through Colombia and Ecuador, climbing the more interesting peaks en route. But these were disappointing after the beauty and adventure we had known in the Sierra Nevada de Santa Marta.

At home again, I found myself thinking constantly of that region—not so much of climbing exploits as of my Indian friends. Had Rosina made a full recovery? What was Atilio doing? I began planning another visit. I read all I could find about the sierra and its people.

The range is a puzzle to geologists. Some believe it is an outlier of the Andes. Others think it is independent of them, a remnant of the ancient Antillean land mass.

At its feet lies the oldest European city in South America that is still inhabited today: Santa Marta, founded in 1525 as a Spanish colony. The harbor here is the busiest on Colombia's north coast; today Santa Marta is a major port for the shipping of bananas, as well as a resort famed for the luxurious beaches nearby.

Before the conquest, the coast and the sierra were populated by independent aboriginal groups—maybe several hundred thousand people in all. With war clubs and poisoned arrows, the coastal tribes fiercely resisted the Spaniards; but they were defeated, tribe by tribe, and pressed into plantation labor. Zealous missionaries sought to end their religious practices. Remnants of the vanquished tribes fled to join those of the sierra.

Meanwhile the Spaniards heard of a people rich in gold, the Tairona, whose fantastic cities of hewn stone lay to the east in the densely forested foothills. A Spanish force glimpsed such a city, marveling at the skill of its stonemasons, its terraced cornfields irrigated by water diverted from mountain streams, and the gift presented by its leaders—by one report, fine gold worth more than 80,000 pesos. If these warlike Indians freely offered so much gold, how much more they must have hidden away!

Years of conflict ensued. By 1600 the Tairona were finally subjugated, their communities sacked, their crops destroyed, their leaders imprisoned. Survivors retreated into the high country, where they lived in obscurity.

Their descendants, I learned, now form a lineage of the Kogi, one of the three tribes surviving in the sierra. The San'ha live on the eastern flanks, and the Ica population is centered on San Sebastián, south of the snow peaks. The three groups speak related languages and describe their relationship as that of "brothers." They share ancient architectural techniques and textile skills, as well as the framework of a pantheistic religion. Their world is peopled by a complex array of male and female spirits, some benign and some downright unfriendly. Male spirits inhabit particular mountain peaks; female spirits dwell in bodies of water.

None of these Indians doubt that the archaeological sites found throughout the sierra, and ascribed to the Tairona, are the work of their ancestors or folk of their ancestors' day.

E quipped with background knowledge—and color film—I returned to the Santa Martas in December 1975. The lure of the snow peaks was still strong; friends I had met in New Hampshire joined me to celebrate the Bicentennial with some climbing. At Valledupar we secured official *permisos* that legitimized our visit for all but those who count most: the Indians themselves. Warned that the villagers of Donachui were turning strangers back, we made our way west to the tribal seat called San Sebastián or, by the Ica, Nabusimake. Three days' trekking with mules took us to the foot of the snow peaks.

In superb weather, I ascended Cristóbal Colón with Lisa Pumpelly and Dan Savage. Dan and I tackled the north face of Pico Guardián; like our diplomat predecessors, we were trapped in cloud at the summit, but we boiled soup and stayed put until visibility improved. We earned a grand view, all the way to Venezuela, as well as a dazzling sunset.

And then, alone, I headed for Sogrome. Until now I had been proud to talk of "my Indian friends"; suddenly the phrase had a naive, presumptuous ring to it. Perhaps Rosina had died, and they blamed her death on me. Probably I would meet Indians I did not know. I decided to travel by night, so no one would send me back.

In late afternoon I followed a wide trail up through coffee plantations. Cows and sheep grazed in tall purple grass on the hillsides, and birds chattered at me from the foliage where streams crossed the path. At nightfall I was plodding toward the top of a ridge above the Donachui Valley. I dozed a few hours near the trail, then picked my way along by the light of my headlamp—a small circle wavering in front of my feet on a trail that grew narrower, and dimmer, with smaller trails branching away. By dawn I was outside Sogrome, waiting to see if I would find Rosina in her house or a bereaved husband, Faustino, with the children. I approached the door with my heart in my mouth. I announced myself loudly in Spanish.

CALLICORE CLYMENA

POLYCHRUS ACUTIROSTRIS

Tropical zone tenants: An "89" or ochenta y nueve butterfly, branded by nature on its wings, lights upon a leaf; a full-grown lizard, two feet long and clad in bright green mail, clings to the gnarled limb of a tree.

"I'm Jaime, the gringo, here to pay you a visit!" A puppy bounded up, wagging its tail. Inside, clustered around the fire, sat Rosina and three of her children, staring. They spoke little Spanish and I even less Icang, but we exchanged greetings of a sort. Rosina fried eggs and plantains for me while a son fetched Faustino from the fields.

Our reunion was heartening indeed. Faustino told me family news, and took me to his uncle, mamo Juan Bautista, to get my visit approved. The priest knew me at once. I presented some gifts: a shiny new Swiss Army knife; small seashells and bright pebbles, like those I had seen him use for healing; and color photographs I had taken two years before. The pictures, which recorded his healing of Rosina, pleased him most.

Now, with the support of Sogrome's leaders, Juan Bautista as tribal priest and Faustino as *comisario,* or village constable, I could share the life of a strictly traditional society. Faustino's mother, Juanita Villafaña, invited me to stay with her and her son Adalberto; I accepted. At night we slept on the dirt floor near the fire. They had cowhides and sheepskins; I, the sleeping bag they called my "cocoon." At dawn we rose to a cup of delicious coffee sweetened with golden chunks of raw sugar. Juanita's family owned large stands of coffee and sugarcane close by, producing more of both than the household could want. The sale of such surplus gives many Ica families their only cash income.

After a breakfast of vegetable stew, I went off with Adalberto to work the farflung fields, some more than an hour's walk from the village. We used machetes to weed and harvest a wide variety of crops, including corn, plantains, and yucca. Sometimes we took food wrapped in plantain leaves and stayed after dark to hunt garden-raiders—the wily *loche,* or brocket deer, and agoutis, the large spotted rodents called *guaras.*

Juanita's immediate family of eight, I learned, was spread about the sierra, managing distant herds and properties. Her husband, the famous mamo José de Jesús, was off planting sugarcane four days' walk to the west. Every week or so, a nephew would arrive at Sogrome, bringing us meat from higher in the mountains or oranges from below. At departure the visitor's mule would be loaded with Sogrome produce. Eventually I saw a pattern in this coming and going, and the economic system became clear.

Families have dispersed through the massif, establishing outposts in various climatic zones. Each zone produces a different set of crops; and land unsuited to farming, such as the paramo above 10,000 feet, serves as pasture. So that everyone may have a balanced diet, foods are redistributed among members of the extended family. The job of transporting foodstuffs by mule naturally falls to the young men, who have the strength for it. This also lets them report news, leave home when parents become overbearing, and see young ladies in distant villages.

Gradually I learned the network of trails. I visited houses scattered in the hills, with gifts of needles for the women, who invariably gave me food, and medicines for the ailing. I acquired the nickname "mamo Jaime."

In mid-March the rainy season altered the rhythm of life. Minor streams became raging waterfalls, and stretches of trail simply washed away. Adalberto, Juanita, and I spent most of our time indoors. I helped Adalberto take his loom in from the rain and prop it against a mud wall. Perched there on a low wooden stool, he wove day and night for more than a week, making himself a new suit with techniques unchanged for generations. They had become second nature to him; he had learned to weave at his father's knee, for among the Ica weaving is the work of men.

Noticing that the striped pattern on the loom matched that of the tunic he was wearing, I asked, "Do you always use the same design?" He spat coca juice on the floor and exclaimed, "*¡Qué va!* This stripe is mine! Always three pairs, here, here, and here." He pointed to his neck and shoulders.

"You never tire of it?" He scowled his answer: No.

Seated on a sheepskin by the fire, Juanita looked up at my preposterous question. Her nimble fingers, holding a top-like wooden spindle, transformed the blob of wool on her lap into a length of strong, uniformly thick yarn. A lifetime of spinning and making bags from unwoven netting, the crafts of women, had taught her aged hands to think for themselves. *"Mamo Jaime quiere saber todos,"* she remarked, smiling— "Mamo Jim wants to know everythings."

It was true. Often I sat up late with mamo Juan Bautista, who told me of tribal history. About 1915, the Ica had asked the President of Colombia for language instructors to teach them Spanish so they could not be cheated easily by outsiders. The teachers who came were missionaries, whose zeal for making converts provoked dissension. Some Ica professed Christianity; others moved to Donachui, to live by the familiar ways.

In June the skies began to clear, and my old friend Atilio arrived one day. He offered to take me up to the high pasture at Mamancanaca, and then to meet his father, José de Jesús Villafaña, a mamo of great distinction.

Our muddy trail was new to me, and amazingly steep. Hour after hour we climbed through tangled forest vegetation until the paramo scrub opened before us.

At about 12,000 feet on a windblown pass, we came upon a cairn, one sharp stone pointing skyward from the center of a circle of smaller stones. This, said Atilio, was an altar to Aruaviku, a major deity. *"Mira allá*—look there," he commanded, pointing to the highest visible summit. "There is the home of Aruaviku, in the red stone." Taking leaves from his *zijew,* or coca bag, he held them to his forehead before dropping them on the altar. "Here is *very* sacred," he said. "If we pass here, it is necessary to pay the god." From this pass, the trail dropped to follow a streambed westward between two huge lateral moraines. Deposited by an ancient glacier as it melted and shrank, these immense piles of boulders and crushed rock ran parallel for miles before us, apparently converging at the horizon.

Folk of the sierra: An Ica father cuddles a baby before leaving to ride west from Pantano to fields he cultivates near Santo Domingo.

We walked, it seemed, with tidal waves of stone poised overhead.

At sunset we sighted Mamancanaca, highest of the Villafaña outposts, where cattle and horses, sheep and goats, roam freely up to the snowline. The plantains we brought were received gladly, and we settled down to plates of mutton and potatoes seasoned with scallions, all fried in animal fat. For several days I helped with the shearing; for several nights I slept in the storehouse, under butchered carcasses hanging from the rafters.

Then we resumed our arduous trek, towed by two self-willed sheep, gifts to the relatives at Prosperidad. These sturdy animals slowed us down so much that we had to stop for the night near San Sebastián. I met Atilio's older brother, Celso, who studied dentistry at hospitals in Valledupar and Santa Marta. Many of his patients were traditionalists, but he wore western clothing and short hair, spoke Spanish perfectly, and carried on his practice with a pedal-driven drill. By lucky timing I also saw the *fiesta* of San Juan Bautista—a religious festival for the Christian Ica, a social occasion for others—before I took up my pack for the last half-day's walk to Prosperidad, an area named for its fertile soil.

Works of a lost society emerge from the roadless jungle of the Buritaca Valley, where circular stone foundations mark housesites of a major Tairona Indian city. Studied by archaeologists since 1975, the "Lost City" sheltered more than 3,000 people for nearly a millennium. But by 1600 gold-hungry Spaniards had plundered and razed every Tairona settlement, erasing the northern sierra's most advanced culture. Surviving Tairona relics may link them to the Ica: Religious carvings adorn a six-foot-long boulder, perhaps a bench for Tairona wayfarers, near Prosperidad in the southern region home to the Ica tribe.

There, at last, I stood face to face with a wizened old man, dressed in tattered white, his machete beside his bare feet. For a long moment he stared at me. "Jaime," he said finally, "I have been waiting for you."

For weeks I accompanied mamo José de Jesús, helping him work his crops. He showed me ancient petroglyphs on boulders along the trails, and sacred *pozos* or bathing spots at the river. At night, swaying in our hammocks, we talked for hours in the dark, and he did his best to explain Ica mythology in his limited Spanish.

One day he showed me his *seguranzas*—archaeological stone figurines, and sacred objects made of wood—and demonstrated their use in divination. Holding a small white cotton bag, which contained stone beads of Tairona origin, José de Jesús tapped it on a miniature wooden stool, summoning a spirit. In a high warbling falsetto, he intoned the spirit's name, bidding him come and sit for consultation. I tape-recorded this, and other incantations, along with the mamo's pungent comments on the disappearance of these songs.

"Now it is all ending," he lamented. "Young people today don't know these songs, they have never heard them. These days it's *chicote* [dance music played on the accordion], that's all. You play these songs for them, you'll see. Not even my son Atilio knows them!"

Then and there I dedicated myself to the task of documenting the Ica way of life, a task which seems to have no end. On three subsequent visits I lived and traveled with my Ica friends, photographing, filming, recording.

I have often asked myself what their fate will be when the surrounding lowlands are fully developed. Colombian law protects the Indians' lands, but what protection can there be for the distinctive cultures that have survived so long in this secluded region?

In the summer of 1981 I returned to the Santa Martas with my wife, Diana, and my brother, Peter. At last I could introduce part of my family to the Villafañas—who had taken me in, against all Ica precedent.

And I showed Diana and Peter one practice that is new. When I first came to the mountains, many Villafaña men owned portable radios. Now they buy cassette recorders instead. Another step toward cultural disintegration? Just the opposite. To the delight of José de Jesús, his sons are no longer listening to Colombian rock and roll on the radio, but recording tribal music and song, and carrying it with them throughout the sierra.

Southernmost snow peak of the group, El Guardián rises 18,000 feet; a glacier hugs its base (opposite). The mountain earns its name guarding the Río Donachui pass, a major route to the central heights. From there, Jim Billipp and Bill McKinney trekked to the south face of Ojeda in early 1974; there, McKinney led an ascent of its sun-dried granite wall (left). Two years later, Billipp saluted America's Bicentennial on the highest summit, Pico Colón. His camera points toward La Reina, and a cloud-covered Venezuela.

OVERLEAF: *A cloud-dotted Caribbean lies beyond the northern summits. Here alpine slopes and lake-dappled valleys—carved by glaciers—lure avid climbers. The Ica hold this region sacred. They deem it the womb of all creation and home to scores of ruling spirits.*

Elderly but agile José de Jesús Villafaña, an Ica mamo, *or priest, prepares to vault the Río Fundación en route to his house at Prosperidad. An agave-fiber sack, slung from his brow by a strap, bulges with produce harvested in a family plot. Skilled farmers, the Ica grow crops suited to various elevations in the southern sierra; those living in one zone exchange food with kin in others, thus strengthening family ties and ensuring a balanced diet. Plantains (above, right) rank as the staple, papayas (above, lower right) as a delicacy. Corn flourishes up to 8,000 feet; in-laws of José de Jesús tend a plot by the Río Donachui at Sogrome (opposite)—and on occasion visit him and tell the family news.*

Walls of unmortared stone corral horses and frame fields of potatoes and scallions on a Villafaña holding at

11,000 feet. Relatives take turns working at this highest of Ica settlements.

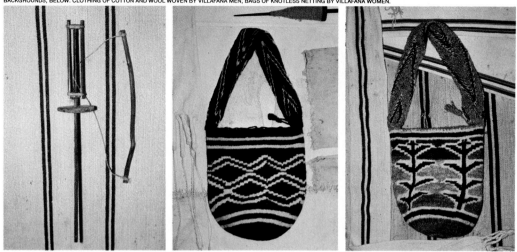

Laying a warp of paired cotton and wool, Faustino Villafaña prepares to weave a tunic. In Ica society, only men weave; women spin thread and make bags by netting. His mother, Juanita, plaits agave fibers into a strap for the bag beside her. She made the woolen bags above, decorating them with the mountain and tree motifs. Men and women alike make use of the bow-driven spindle (above, left) to make rope.

125

Chores done, José de Jesús relaxes with a grandson at Prosperidad. For enjoyment, the mamo chews the mildly narcotic leaves of coca—a practice common in cultures of the Andes, and restricted to married males by Ica tradition. He uses a stick to take lime from a gourd full of powdered seashells; lime enhances coca's stimulating effect. His son Adalberto, at his mother's Sogrome home, fashions sandals from tire treads as a friend looks on. Before cutting the rubber, he walks the tread to measure foot length. Winding a leather thong through the sole completes the job. A loom stands nearby; the Ica, a society of accomplished weavers, believe that the practice of this ancient art helps sustain the cosmic order.

Parading a statue of St. John the Baptist through San Sebastián, Ica in western or traditional dress open the annual Fiesta de San Juan—more holiday than holy day to the non-Christian majority. A white-bearded Roman Catholic priest from the nearby Capuchin mission directs the procession. Alone in a large kankurua, *or men's ceremonial house, mamo Antonio Crespo practices ritual flute music. Men who seek counsel would sit on the low stools and bring offerings that include cotton thread, which represents the umbilical cord. Burial rites for a young girl at Sogrome also involve an umbilical symbol. A friend of the grieving father ties an agave string leading from the corpse to a branch stuck in the ground above the grave; when this fiber disintegrates, the child's soul has left the body.*

Arriving for the fiesta, an Ica couple heads for the "doorway" —a narrow ladder propped against the village wall. The thatch-topped east gate has stood closed ever since many Ica, at odds with local missionaries, abandoned this tribal seat more than 50 years ago. A few live here now; others return only to tend gardens, or on ceremonial occasions. Pride in their way of life remains fervent— the man carries a tape unit on which he will record tribal music.

The Alpujarras

By Tor Eigeland
Photographs by the Author

The whiff of fragrance was tantalizing. I pulled the car off the narrow road, got out, and stepped away from it. Now the air was an intoxicating, invigorating perfume. Thyme and rosemary I could distinguish. The rest was a blend of flowers, mixed with the scent of pines and damp earth. Burbling, dripping sounds of water joined with goat- and sheep-bells in a happy symphony accented by what the local people call *cañones*—literally, cannon; in fact, deep, booming cowbells.

Above me, slanting afternoon rays of warm sunlight bathed the green fields carved as terraces into the abrupt slopes of the Poqueira Canyon, and three gleaming white villages, their rectangular houses fitted together tightly, clung to the hillside. For a moment it suggested Indonesia. But from the north the jagged snow-topped peak called El Veleta looked down from a haughty summit of 11,129 feet, proof that I was indeed in the Alpujarras, a region practically unknown even to many Spaniards.

I had learned some particulars. The frosty Sierra Nevada peaks form a northern limit, while the southern reaches end in the subtropical waters of the Mediterranean, on the Costa del Sol. To the east, the Alpujarra runs to the Sierra de Gádor, and on the west to the Sierra de Lújar and the town of Lanjarón. Nearly three-fourths of it—the most obviously scenic parts—fall within Granada Province; the rest, sere and hilly, lies in Almería. Today the inhabitants number about 60,000. They often distinguish the Alpujarra Alta, the high country, from the Alpujarra Baja, the lower, and the name may appear in the singular or in the plural without upsetting anyone. But nothing had prepared me for this moment.

On a curve just above this splendid overlook, a big sign announced: "PAMPANEIRA, ALPUJARRA. *Viajero, quédate a vivir con nosotros.*" That is, "Traveler, stay here and live with us."

It was like magic from the beginning: that first panorama, and the scents, and this sign—innocent of translations for tourists—which made me feel welcome. Lodging is scant in the Alpujarras, but the Hostal Pampaneira found me a spotless and cheerful room, and I strolled next door to a little bar. These small bars, along with little plazas and the flat roofs of the houses in good weather, constitute the social centers of the region; and I wanted to compare impressions with those of Granada's poet José G. Ladrón de Guevara. He says, of the Alpujarrans: "What good people,/ they speak slowly,/ look you straight in the eye."

Loud conversation was buzzing in the plain, white-painted room. I asked for a *vinillo,* a small glass of the local wine, and it came with bread

In sunshine warm as her smile, María López Perez peeks through peppers and an ancient grapevine on her balcony in Mecina Fondales. Called by one writer "the eye of the house," balconies in Spain's Alpujarras ensure privacy, yet permit sociability.

Rumpled landscape, the Alpujarras slope south from Spain's snowy Sierra Nevada to the Mediterranean. The region has attracted diverse invaders, including Greeks, Romans, Visigoths, and Arabs. Between 711 and 1550 the Moors prospered here, but economic decline followed the Christian reconquest. Since 1960 the population has fallen from 70,000 to about 60,000 as people emigrate to find work.

and a slice of the famous cured ham of the region. While sipping the wine, which looks like rosé but has a strong, fruity taste, I counted 92 hams hanging from the chestnut beams of the ceiling.

Most of the customers were men, lean, wiry, gentle in manner. Older men wore their traditional narrow-brimmed dark hats; others had removed them, revealing a startling white from the bridge of the nose upward, in sharp contrast to the red-brown from the sun. Two *locos* were making quite a lot of cheerful noise, ignored but accepted by the rest.

"Don't touch me, I'll spill over!" a man next to me warned his friend. "And me too," replied the other. "I have a chestnut big as a piano." For some odd reason, here "to have" or "to carry" a chestnut means to be drunk. I certainly would not have thought they were drunk; and many customers were having coffee.

I had to ask the owner to repeat what I owed. "Thirty pesetas." He smiled. "Do you think it's too much?" "No, no. I thought it would be more." I left in disbelief: less than one American dollar for two glasses of wine and two slices of that delicious ham, celebrated for centuries.

Trevélez, the highest town in Spain, is the ham capital of the Alpujarras. Early one morning I made the winding half-hour drive from Pampaneira. Stopping for everything worth looking at can lengthen the trip to a day: I only paused to admire a backlit cluster of some forty chestnut trees in full bloom and to watch a man operating a steam-roller—with a red carnation held between his teeth.

Antonio Gonzalez Alvarez, a big, blondish man with hamlike arms, was feeding his brood sows when I arrived. The squealing and grunting that pervaded the sty drove us into the open to talk. I had learned that most people raise pigs for family consumption only, yet some 120,000 cured hams leave the Alpujarras every year. I asked Don Antonio to explain.

"Some buy young pigs from the outside, to raise them and slaughter them here. But—and this is more profitable—many simply buy hams from big producers elsewhere for curing here." "Then what is the secret of that great flavor?" "Air-drying—our air is dry, clean and healthy. We don't use refrigeration chambers. People say we cure the ham in the snow. This is not really true, though it does snow a lot in winter."

Politely, but firmly, Don Antonio excused himself: "Gotta work.

Come back any time and we'll have a vinillo. *Que vaya usted con Dios*—May you go with God." Alpujarran speech, which discards the letter "s," contracts the farewell into a blurry parting shot: mayougowigaw.

And so I did, through a town which cascades down the hillside from nearly 5,600 feet at the highest house to almost 5,000 at the lowest. On the way I stopped to see a man well known as Don Federo Eldelamiel— Theoneofthehoney. The Alpujarra is famous for its fine honey, and Don Federo was supposed to have the best of all. He was not home; but his wife, a handsome middle-aged woman in traditional black, let me in.

"Yes, we have the best honey!" She was pleased that I had heard. "Have a taste!" She dipped her finger into a big container and let honey drip onto my finger, remarking, "I've just washed my hands." I licked my finger. Surely this *was* the best. And while she filled two jars for me, I asked what they did with the bees in winter when snow covered everything. "In September," she told me, "we load all the hives onto a truck and take them down to La Rábita, on the Alpujarran coast." This coast in January has the highest average temperature in Spain: nearly 60°F.

Another "mayougowigaw," and I was strolling down through narrow alleys between whitewashed walls. Now and then mules with enormous saddlebaskets, taking up all the space there was, forced me into a doorway or a different alley; they carry all sorts of things, from produce to stone. Women, alone or with a friend or two, sat outside their houses on very small chairs, knitting or embroidering or mending or peeling potatoes. Invariably they would look up and greet the stranger cheerfully, without shyness, in their soft, sweet, singsongy accent: "*Buenodía . . . Adióo . . .* Mayougowigaw." The poet, clearly, had described them aright.

I n the lower town I met God's representative, the priest Don José Peinado Martínez, for lunch at a plain table-and-chairs restaurant. Everyone greeted Don José, and the coltish, quick-witted young waitress set wine and slices of ham before us. Then crusty new bread. The food of the Alpujarras is so fresh it seems to sparkle.

A stocky, fair-skinned man of 34, Don José has green eyes that flash with intelligence and humor. He obviously loves his work, his rather earthy parishioners, and the Alpujarras in general. While we ate, he regaled me with stories. When he first arrived, he said, he went to the barber's. The barber asked: "You want it cheap or expensive?" "I just want a haircut." "If I cut it in the sun it is cheaper. In the shade it is more expensive. Because of the shade." And why should a haircut be priced like a seat at the bullfight? Just one of those things.

Don José told me about nicknames, *apodos,* which had already complicated my visit. Again and again I would arrive in a town, asking for someone by the full name, and people would give me a blank stare. After a thorough description of, say, Juan Gonzalez, someone would say: "Ah, you mean Juan Guardarrío [Watchriver]." In one case I was told: "Oh—Matasuegra [the Mother-in-Law Killer]." (In fact, he had only beaten her up.)

"Here just about everyone has been 'confirmed,' or given a nickname," said Don José. "The reason may be that last as well as first names are very common. Most nicknames are descriptive, like Juan el Sordo—the Deaf. Some refer to a profession: Miguel the Shoemaker, Juana the Miller. The best are satirical, like Trepalitros, 'Spill-liters' around here, for one who drinks too much. Some are inherited and may have lasted for centuries, like

Los Nuestros [The Ours], Los Jesusa, Los Tutos. And we don't know the origin of many of these. One of my favorites is El Humedades [Humidities]. It's for the guy who looks after the *acequias,* the irrigation canals. He always has his pants rolled up and his feet are invariably wet!"

I had a favorite to tell: "Around Soportújar there used to be a man called Juan the Hare. It seems that his grandfather once found himself stuck with some friends at mealtime. He told them: 'Come and have some cat with tomato. It's delicious! You've never tried it? Oh, come on!' His friends couldn't bring themselves to eat cat, and Juan ate it all himself.

Well, it wasn't cat, but a tasty hare. For two generations that name clung to the family."

Don José guffawed. "But," he warned me, "don't ever use a nickname to anyone's face. It gives offense—except sometimes with the ones that are centuries old."

Tradition and a feeling of mystery pervade the Alpujarra. There is a legend of love or war or supernatural events clinging to nearly every corner, canyon, or hilltop. Almost all the place-names are evocative: Ravine of the Blood, or Gorge of the Treasure. Arab components are usually the most recent: Rambla de la Alcazaba—Arroyo of the Fortress; La Mezquita—the Mosque.

On the third try I found the hilltop called La Mezquita: east along the road from Mecina Fondales, down the fields past the mulberry trees, along the canal, "the one with all the trees and bushes." I was standing in a clearing with a stunning view. Below me ran the canyon of the Río Trevélez, its hillsides varied by stands of wheat, corn, barley, rye, beans, and tomatoes. Groves of poplar, chestnut, and almond trees climbed the slopes and lined the riverbanks. The stream raced along under an old bridge, perhaps of Moorish date. On the far side, vineyards and rocky, ancient mule trails climbed the hill called La Corona. Behind that loomed the Sierra de Contraviesa, screening the Mediterranean from my gaze.

Laden with the land's bounty, the Alvarez sisters head for their house in Mecina Fondales. More than 80 percent of Alpujarrans live by agriculture, cultivating kitchen gardens as well as outlying fields to feed their families.

Before me, about 500 yards down to the left, was a round stone platform, an *era,* or threshing floor. A pair of mules were walking around and around it, pulling a boy standing on a sled-like contraption. Obviously he was a Roman soldier in a chariot, charging the enemy! Shouting, cracking his whip, he failed to impress the mules much. This method of threshing must be thousands of years old; some of the "sleds" have stones on the underside to cut the grain, while others use steel wheels.

Near me stood a rambling old farmhouse, now used as an animal shelter. An irrigation canal brought it a dribble of rainwater.

Just a few yards beyond the house I found a platform, stone upon stone, quite large enough to hold a small mosque. One point of it was aligned eastward, toward Mecca. This is the sort of airy site, with a good view, that the Moors liked. But then, they were not the only ones who liked such a vista, and I found no trace of an upper structure at all.

I asked several local farmers about La Mezquita, and they all gave me exactly the same reply: "They say the Moors used to have a mosque there.

That's what my father told me and his grandfather said the same thing."

One authority, author and publisher Francisco Izquierdo, told me he thought the place was much, much older; that the foundation of the platform dated from Roman times, or perhaps from a Greek colony, Ulisea, hereabouts. There were plans, he said, to excavate the site.

At the cost of destroying an unspoiled, singularly restful spot, such a dig might unearth traces of many of the peoples that settled in the region.

Of the first inhabitants—hunting tribes of uncertain origins—little is known; their tiny flint blades are found in coastal rock shelters. Later folk developed a Neolithic culture, keeping cattle and sheep and goats, growing lentils and barley and peas, weaving cloth and making pottery. By 3000 B.C. they had learned how to work the copper ores of the area.

Rich mineral deposits, including gold and silver, attracted Phoenician and Greek settlers and the merchant-warrior Carthaginians. When the Punic Wars shook southern Spain, men from the Alpujarra may well have fought with Hannibal's Carthaginians against the Romans; after the Roman victory they held a fierce pocket of resistance against the new rulers. From that day to this, they have shown a similar, stubborn conservatism.

Christianity arrived; the Roman Empire in the west broke up; other invaders entered Spain. The Visigoths came, conquered, and quarreled among themselves until by A.D. 700 Spain was divided and disaffected, ripe for the plucking. In July 710 the first Arab reconnaissance force landed near Gibraltar; about a year later came the first major Arab victory. Within a decade or so Spain was virtually a Muslim domain, including the Alpujarra—to the extent that these independent, rebellious people ever accepted anything from the outside.

Prosperity came to them after 955, from Almería, the ancient port city refounded by the Arabs and renamed. The city's looms produced silk in abundance—and the slopes of the Alpujarras were ideal for the cultivation of mulberry trees, the leaves of which are the favorite food of the silkworm. As the silk industry expanded, Berbers from the North African mountains flocked into the Alpujarras, terracing their fields and planting vegetables, digging their famous irrigation canals, and building in the style still visible in the region. Apparently they became the majority; certainly their way of life prevailed.

Now agriculture and mining thrived alike. Gold- and silversmiths and other artisans plied their trades in the towns while mule skinners scrambled up and down the trails with their wares. Ships carried silk to Italy, and across the Mediterranean; camel caravans trudged across the Sahara, taking silk to the great trading centers of black Africa.

In the Alpujarras, it was said, even the poorest wore silk garments.

Yet, after centuries, the Muslims of Spain were losing their strongholds to Christian forces. On November 25, 1491, Ferdinand and Isabella, the Catholic monarchs, signed a treaty with Muhammad XII, better known as Boabdil, the last emir of Granada. Extremely generous to the

Weighing in at 400 pounds, Trevélez hams will command a high price in Granada and earn income for some in the cash-poor Alpujarras. Joaquín Gonzalez Alvarez cures the flavorful delicacy—famous for centuries—in clean mountain air.

Moors, the terms included marked respect for their property and their religion. Boabdil himself was given a seigneury in the Alpujarras.

On January 2, 1492, Boabdil surrendered the Alhambra. He and his household rode off toward his vestige of a realm. At a pass still called Suspiro del Moro, the Sigh of the Moor, he turned in his saddle for the last look at lovely Granada—and eight hundred years! Apparently he wept. According to legend, his mother, Ayesha, gave him a stinging epitaph: "Weep like a woman for what you could not defend like a man."

Still a young man, he lingered in the high country. Sometimes he spent weeks in the open, hunting hares with greyhounds and small birds with goshawks. Then his beloved wife Moraima died; and in the fall of 1493 he and his retinue set sail for Morocco, where he died dishonored.

In Spain, all too soon, Christian authorities were violating the rights of the Moors—and uprisings flared repeatedly in the Alpujarras. The Moriscos, professed Christians of Moorish descent and culture, suffered special humiliations. The chronicler Luis del Mármol Carvajal, who was there in the 1560s, reported the extortions practiced by Christian officials stationed at Ugíjar, then as now one of the principal Alpujarran towns. Most of these men had wives and families in Granada. They would go home for holidays with chickens, honey, fruit, and money from the farmhouses along the way—things "they would take from the Moriscos any way they could."

After 1550 a ban on the export of silks threatened the whole economy; and in 1567 Moorish customs and the speaking of Arabic were prohibited,

all books and legal documents in Arabic being declared forfeit or invalid.

At Juviles, in the very heart of the Alpujarra, where people had a reputation for being fierce, a major rebellion began. In 1568 a Morisco from the town of Válor was named king, as Aben Humeya—that is, Ibn Umayya—and the fires spread quickly. Christians who did not deny their faith were tormented and tortured, and sometimes killed. Priests were often the victims; churches were profaned. Not until late 1570 could the forces of Philip II, after savage fighting, finally gain the day for the Christian cause.

The cost to the region of Granada, especially the Alpujarras, was extremely high. The Moriscos were exiled. New settlers were brought into an area mangled by war, Christian farmers from other parts of Spain. They faced brigands in the hills, pirates on the coast, and iron-fisted officials in the towns. They knew how to grow grain—their descendants still grow grain—but this is not an ideal crop for the abrupt Alpujarran slopes. The Alpujarra escaped total ruin, but it faded into obscurity, never to recapture the glory it had shared in the days of the Moors.

But the presence of the Moors is still felt, not only in concrete things like the irrigation system, the cultivation of mulberry trees, the architecture of the houses, the sweets relished at the crowning of Ibn Umayya and the fiestas of today. They are given credit, locally, for anything old or of uncertain origin, such as ruins and bridges. People still tell tales about the days of the Moors, children learn about them from the history books, and the radio may pick up a North African broadcast as often as a Spanish one. Everyone makes a point of telling you that on a very clear day, from high ground, you can look south across the Mediterranean and see the Rif Mountains—"the mountains of the Moors"—in the distance.

To this day, noisy battles are waged between Moors and Christians in the towns of the Alpujarras, during the fiestas of *"moros y cristianos."* The best, I was told, is that of Válor.

I t really starts on the afternoon of September 14, for this is the feast of the Holy Christ of the Ivy, the Patron of Válor. *"¡Viva el Santo Cristo de Válor!"* The shout goes up. Thousands of voices reply: *"¡VIVA!"* To a steady, unrelenting drumbeat and the ear-splitting bursts of rockets and fireworks, the great crucifix is brought out of the church and paraded through the town. On this day the Christ wears a crown of gold and—for some reason—a skirt, which not even the parish priest could explain. From both sides men steady the statue with long poles.

Religious and civil notables, and bands of musicians, march in the procession. The entire route is lined by men, women, and children, many holding lighted candles. Outside every private home the owner, if he has any pride, sets off his own private fireworks. The procession stops; it has to. It resumes. Then the statue inches, dips and rocks forward, lower, lower, lower—the crowd holds its breath—to pass under some electric wires.

Toward the rear of the procession, with solemnity, marches a troop of Christian soldiers decked out in 16th-century style—but no Moors.

As I watched the return of the Cristo de Válor to the church, three hours (or one mile) later, another tremendous volley of noisemakers and rockets, a whole plaza full, was set off. "Not bad for a small town," I shouted to a dark gypsy who was wearing a jaunty cap and a branch of basil behind his ear. He laughed: "If we don't make a *lot* of noise we just don't feel we have honored our Cristo right."

At dozens of stands, itinerant vendors were selling Morisco sweets, cheap plastic toys, firecrackers, soaps, and perfumes. People bought beer and wine in plenty from an enormous stand beside the church, but I only saw one drunk, and he looked like a chronic case. At sunset many strolled

Nose in a comic book, a young Alpujarran girl rides a mule's rumble seat. Dark-eyed Luz María Martín charms with a winsome smile. Though health and education have improved since the 1950s, the lack of jobs and the difficulties of marginal farming continue to drive young Alpujarrans away from the region.

Summer brings a profusion of flowers and fruit to the Alpujarras. Sweet cherries weigh down branches in an orchard. A butterfly sips nectar from a "widow's flower." Evening brings out a magenta-colored "four-o'clock." Delicate petals of a wild caper spread to the sun. A few local people collect its buds for pickling.

off to a dance, while others stood around talking and laughing and drinking wine until late, late in the night.

Not until about eleven the next morning did Válor stir back to life. Both Moors and Christians in costume joined ordinary citizens for coffee with milk. But soon the time-steeped plaza became a center of activity. Facing it stood a wood-framed "castle" of canvas, where the Christian king took his place with an ambassador and other officials. The Christian general and soldiery were assembled in front of it. Now the full drama began, in grand and formal verse. I can only suggest the style in English prose.

After some preliminary ceremony a terrified Christian spy appears, hesitating to break the bad news. The king urges him to speak. He declaims: "I am going to tell you, as this is the sole reason for my coming. A moment ago I found myself in the towers of Balerma, when I saw appearing, in the wide ocean, fine sailing ships rigged for war. The proud Half-Moon, sir, was flying ostentatiously among them, and I could make out, through the dawn, in the quivering reflections, that all of them were full of arms and Moors."

PRUNUS AVIUM — SWEET CHERRY

"What?" The king sends his general to verify this report, with the splendid rhetoric that dignifies the drama. The townspeople shape its words with their lips, knowing it by heart, loving it.

Worst fears confirmed, the general returns. A Moorish ambassador, wearing a turban, arrives on horseback and claims a hearing: "Listen for a moment, Christian king, and you will know what brings me. After long years of terrible wars, bloody and horrid battles, Ferdinand the Catholic Monarch and his wife hurled us out of our native homes. There was not a corner in the flowery plain of Granada unwashed by Morisco blood, and in our defeat we had to suffer the saddest of public outrages."

The ambassador demands the surrender of the castle. After sharp rebukes condemning this affront to Spain and to Christianity, the Christian king sends him packing, and now there is war.

Armed with shotguns loaded with blanks, Moorish and Christian soldiers fill the plaza. They fire as fast as they can load, and the din is enough to leave the ears ringing 24 hours later.

In the morning war, the Moors win; they occupy the castle. After lunch, siestas, and more libations, the conflict resumes. Dialogue in a lighter key precedes actual combat. One Moor captures a Christian spy, roughs him up, and tries to convert him: "Furthermore, we have just as many women as we like. You yourself, if you have such ambitions, can have A HUNDRED!"

Glumly, the Christian answers: "What kind of an advantage is that? Let me tell you, with the one I got, I am in hell most of the time, and I know that if I had any more, they would skin me alive!"

The Moor argues on, praising his homeland: "There you will spend your life between music and festivities." And the spy retorts: "But I wouldn't be drinking wine—a thing which *here,* Moor, I do plenty!"

Of course the Christians win the afternoon campaign. In the end the Moorish king is converted to Christianity, and the two sovereigns embrace.

Thundering applause follows. And then everyone celebrates some more, in a happy, relaxed fashion. Generosity reigns. I found myself a guest at meals, and over cups of coffee. The hospitality was certainly Moorish!

Yet today the Alpujarra is a poor region—materially. True, it has escaped the misery of the past. I had read of hard times in Gerald Brenan's classic book *South From Granada*. As a young Englishman, poor himself, he lived in the town of Yegen in the 1920s; he has been in and out of the Alpujarra ever since, and has captured its true quality. I had the privilege of meeting "Don Geraldo," and we talked of the days when "there weren't any cars, there weren't any roads, there was hardly a bathroom in the whole of the Alpujarras. Now all the better-off farmers have baths."

ARGYNNIS SP. (FRITILLARY) ON TRACHELIUM CAERULEUM— FLOR DE LA VIUDA, OR WIDOW'S FLOWER

This noted author gave me a warning, as we discussed the changes he has seen: "You can't read about the Alpujarras—a bit about the history and that's it. You just have to talk to people about it."

I thought of a tale I had heard, "from my mother's time" or "my grandmother's day"—how gypsies used to earn a coin or two from people too poor to have meat of their own. The gypsies would arrive with a hambone on a string, *el saboré,* and dip it into the stewpot for as long as the housewife could afford, to add flavor to the beans or lentils. No more.

Still, the once-booming mining business is practically dead: "The mine is here, yes. But the work, no." The silkworms no longer spin their cocoons, and many of the mulberry trees have been cut down. The growing of cereals on the tricky slopes, the reaping with a sickle, the transportation by mule and packbasket—anything but profitable. And the young have been leaving in droves, to seek work as far away as Germany.

MIRABILIS JALAPA—"FOUR-O'CLOCK"

To consult an authority on how Alpujarrans currently make a living, I went to Pórtugos, a traditional little town with disarming claims to fame. It has mineral springs with six different flavors of medicinal waters; two extremely pretty girls; Don Miguel and his wife, América, who run a bar and keep some of the finest wine in the region for their friends; and Dr. Francisco Puertas Prieto, a soft-spoken young man who is vet for the whole district. Our paths had crossed repeatedly, for he travels from farm to farm at a furious pace and is known everywhere, inevitably, as El Veterinario.

CAPPARIS SPINOSA—CAPER

"As you know," he began, "pigs are raised mostly for family consumption. Here you couldn't just go and buy meat in a store. There were wild rabbits and hares as well as partridges for protein, but in 1956 myxomatosis practically wiped out the wild rabbit population.

"Lamb and veal is what they must produce here to make money. Except for family gardens, our farmers should forget the beans and the cereals; they cannot compete with mechanized agriculture in these crops.

"There is fine fruit here—cherries, apples, pears. The walnuts and chestnuts are of excellent quality, and there are lots of almonds. Unfortunately, walnut wood fetched a very good price for a while, so most of the trees were cut down for a quick profit.

"Also, a bit of well-directed tourism might help." We both knew the difficulties here: the tricky roads, the scarcity of petrol stations, the scarcity of lodgings, the language barrier. I was reminded of the last as El Veterinario concluded: "And there is the money sent home by the emigrants." I had heard of Alpujarrans who worked in Germany for ten years and only learned to say *"Ja."*

Yet I met other young people who had come home from well-paid jobs determined to face the hardships of working the land rather than be faceless individuals in ever-nastier, polluted big cities. They spoke of the things that had appealed to me: peace, fresh and fragrant air, clean water, life among good people who care about one another.

"I love the last part of autumn, the winter till December," one man told me. "Rain, clouds right up into the mountains—fantastic tones of light. But January, February, and March are really rough!" I could believe that. One September day on top of the Sierra de Lújar, I was nearly blown off a precipice, and had to crawl on all fours to safety.

I shared some of the chores—and fun—of the grape harvest; and finally

"Like vapor coming out of witches' brew," the author imagined the morning mist—typical of the Alpujarras—rising from valleys of La Contraviesa, below the Sierra de Lújar. Narrow, winding roads, all of them scenic and many of them unpaved, require alert driving even in good weather. "One wrong twist of the wheel," says the author, "and away you go forever!"
Goats find the terrain more suited to their skills and taste, as they browse on precipitous slopes— or block the way.

left the Alpujarras on a clear, lovely fall day. During a last morning walk around the narrow streets of Pampaneira I realized that there were still many corners I had not noticed in this little town—corners with balconies full of flowers, each with individuality. The white walls were covered with red peppers drying for the winter months ahead. In the airy lofts of the houses I could see onions and apples hanging from the ceiling, tied in bunches. They would keep till spring. Partridges, hens, and chicks made clucking noises in their wire cages.

"In personal things," a professional man had told me, "these people are super-reserved. The mouth is closed with seven locks and seven keys." Yet if the stranger observes basic good manners, a smile and courteous *"buenos días"* will open a very hospitable world.

Everywhere people greeted me. At the little hotel I had a late breakfast in the kitchen with the owners, the Martín family. For the past ten days they had not let me eat in the dining room, saying I would fare better in the kitchen. Which was true.

Driving away, I stopped repeatedly to say good-bye. One friend insisted on giving me a bottle of homemade wine, another a bag of almonds, someone else again some apples—for the road. "They speak slowly,/ look you straight in the eye." And easing my car through the last iffy curves of the Alpujarra I realized that whether I returned or not, this magic place was now lodged securely in a big, sunny corner of my soul.

Snow-dusted El Veleta, second highest peak in the region, looms beyond gleaming white Capileira, clinging to the chestnut- and poplar-studded slopes of Barranco de Poqueira. In his 1828 journal, Washington Irving called the Alpujarras "Stern mountains of marble & granite, with here and there a little emerald valley. . . ."

After morning coffee, and perhaps a little brandy, a farmer leads his horse and milch goats to fields outside Trevélez, the highest town in Spain. Houses here—as in other Alpujarran villages—crowd close to the street, veiling windows and balconies with masses of flowering plants. From the security of a rooftop niche, a cat watches for the fish seller from the coast. Nasturtiums and other blossoms encircle a tile-capped chimney in another village. "The Alpujarrans are closed about anything personal," says one resident, "with seven locks and keys." Yet the author, who speaks fluent Spanish, found them warm and welcoming. He could stop "just about anywhere and get into an easy relationship with people."

*"My father was brought up in an oven. . . . I was born in an oven!" exclaims Señora
Josefa Zamorano Ramón. "We have never done anything else." Clad in the black
customary for older women, she weighs out a kilo of dough to assure full measure. Her
daughter Señora Luisa Vasquez Zamorano scores loaves of* pan casero, *home-style bread,
awaiting the wood-burning oven, a Moorish type. The bakery in Capileira produces
about 100 items daily, including elongated rolls and the sweet* torta de lata *flavored with
cinnamon. Author and long-time resident of the region, Gerald Brenan tells how
the Alpujarrans used to revere their daily bread: "Before cutting a new loaf it was
proper to make the sign of the cross over it with a knife." And so they do today.*

Harvesting grapes becomes a family affair for the Martín household and their friends. Autumn-tinged vines sprawl over the ground in the Spanish style at the vineyard near Pampaneira. The types of grapes grown here include a dark or "black" variety and several "whites." Mules haul the fruit to vans that take it to the winepress in Pampaneira. Alpujarran families sometimes move to farmhouses, called cortijos, to harvest crops or to make cheese in summer.

Wine streams from a bota,
or wineskin, to quench the
thirst of Alfredo López
Domingo, a Pampaneira
farmer. The robust
Alpujarran product—a
light-colored wine made
from a combination of dark
and light grapes—serves to
meet local demand and goes
to other markets in southern
Spain. The author, at
center wearing the new
green boots provided by
his hosts, joined in the fun
of the Martíns' annual
grape pressing at
Pampaneira. Well fortified
with samples from previous
years, the "stompers"
crushed grapes for six hours
in the lagar, *or winepress*
room. The juice drained into
a vat; José Martín took it
up by the bucketful and
funneled it into an oak
barrel to age for at least
four months and perhaps
for a decade.

"I am the arm of vengeance!" shouts the Christian king as his soldiers storm the Moorish-held castle in the final segment of Válor's Fiesta de moros y cristianos. *The two-day festival recalls the submission in 1492 of Granada to Their Catholic Majesties, Ferdinand and Isabella. On the first day, villagers carry the golden image of El Cristo de la Yedra, their holy patron, from the church to the plaza and back. Blasting muskets and smoke belie the friendly merriment of the occasion, revealed in the engaging grin of one Christian soldier. After the final Christian victory, Moor and Christian alike find comradery in nearby taverns.*

Ruins of the Castillo de Lanjarón guard the western entry into the Alpujarras. Always a region of resistance, the Alpujarras have offered sanctuary to dissenters well into the 20th century. Even after the fall of Granada, the Moors held out here for another 80 years, until the Castilians crushed their last rebellion. A stone bridge, possibly Moorish, spans the Río Trevélez. Only remnants of the Islamic past remain in the region—a few bridges and castles, and a number of acequias, or irrigation canals.

OVERLEAF: A shepherd guards his charges in a harvested barley field above Capileira.

Frolicking horse merges into afternoon mist, its work hours over. Horses and mules still provide transportation

and help cultivate fields for many Alpujarrans.

The Ruwenzori

By Noel Grove
Photographs by James A. Sugar

Night, like a dark liquid, filled the valleys far below and then crept up the mountainside. The two of us had built a fire to drive back the chill and lonely quiet at nearly 14,000 feet. Our porters had moved downslope for the evening after making it clear that they did not like the heights of the Ruwenzori, Africa's eerie Mountains of the Moon.

Darkness, and the first shrieks, reached us almost simultaneously. The sound resembled a human cry of distress except that it stayed at the same high, keening note, never varying in pitch.

"What do you think it is?" asked photographer Jim Sugar. The screams seemed to come from several directions—below us on the slope, behind us on the glacial melt called Green Lake, above us on Wasuwameso peak, which we planned to scale in the morning.

"It's probably an eagle or a night hawk soaring around the cliffs," I suggested.

The screams continued, high and quavering. We threw more brush on the fire and made thin jokes about driving back the evil forces of the night.

The mind plays tricks when the eyes dwell too long on the bizarre. The Ruwenzori Mountains, on the border between Zaire and Uganda, seem to specialize in the unusual. We had walked that morning through a Grimm's fairyland of gnarled conifers, whose twisted roots interwove our steep path. Lace-like green lichens hung wispy from the trees, and multicolored moss several feet thick carpeted the ground.

About noon we had emerged into an even stranger world of outsize vegetation. Lobelia is known to flower lovers in Europe and America as a plant measured in inches. Now it towered over our heads. Huge groundsels, foot-high weeds in the United States, here could have been cabbages from a garden of giants and we the diminutive visitors from Lilliput.

And hour after hour, the strange silence. Few animals live in these chilly heights. Those that do are in many ways as bizarre as the vegetation. Deep in the moss burrow worms a yard long. Scampering among the rocks at higher elevations are those odd creatures the rock hyraxes. Although hyraxes resemble woodchucks, their closest living relatives are elephants. They announce their feeding time at the end of each day—we learned after our descent—with the high, monotonal shrieks that shattered our campfire calm like a banshee wail.

Daytime was more serene. We walked among the clouds in these mountains, whose name in a local dialect means "rainmaker." Precipitation may exceed 200 inches a year, much of it soaked up by the mossy

On the bleak slopes of Mount Stanley, giant groundsels and white everlastings thrive near Alexandra Glacier in Africa's damp and eerie Ruwenzori—the Mountains of the Moon. Here plants reach bizarre size; groundsels may grow 40 feet tall.

Vigorous geological activity shaped the landforms of eastern Zaire; violent political upheavals marked the nation. Volcanoes still belch smoke and lava in the Virunga Range. The lakes—their Belgian colonial names changed by President Mobutu Sese Seko in 1973—lie in the western arm of the Great Rift Valley. Fault blocks forced upward when the valley sank in the Precambrian Era produced Africa's highest range, the Ruwenzori. These peaks, only 30 miles north of the Equator, run 70 miles along the Zaire-Uganda border. Clouds veil the summits, and more than 200 inches of rain a year drench the highlands.

terrain and released slowly and steadily. Ptolemy wrote in A.D. 150 that the Nile was born in runoff from a range called the Mountains of the Moon.

First outside verification of the Ruwenzori was made by the explorer Henry Stanley. The man who had found Dr. Livingstone is said to have camped several days at the base of these mountains in 1888 without presuming their existence. On the day he left, the screen of clouds parted and revealed, to his astonishment, a majestic snowcapped range.

Still infrequently visited, these mountains are far from unexplored. The highest peaks, some of which exceed 16,000 feet, were climbed and mapped in 1906. Thus ours was an expedition of curiosity, not of conquest, in a region that—nearly a century after Stanley's explorations—keeps a sense of youth. Our road to the Ruwenzori was filled with scenes of promise, frustration, and vistas of primeval beauty.

Our journey began in Bukavu, capital of Zaire's Kivu Province, a place that visiting Americans have called "an African San Francisco." Appealing, solidly built villas overlook the water from four peninsulas that extend into Lake Kivu—but on the slopes behind them sit flimsy, fly-ridden shacks. Such contrasts inflamed the turbulent 1960s, following Zaire's independence after 52 years as the Belgian Congo. Then Africans and European mercenaries clashed in civil wars; some 8,000 Africans and 500 Europeans were killed; and a number of white hostages were executed. Now, as non-African visitors, Jim and I drew friendly attention. To the dozens of French-speaking Zairians that we met all along the way, we were simply *Américains,* objects of sociable curiosity and frequently the recipients of help in case of a mired car or a parched throat.

Near Bukavu, apparently far from politics, we walked in a Garden of Eden. In the face of a fast-growing population and increasing demand for croplands, President Mobutu Sese Seko has set aside thousands of acres as national parks. In verdant Kahuzi-Biega Park, nearly 250,000 acres, we sought those muscular dwellers of the rain forest, the lowland gorillas.

Our small safari consisted of several Pygmy trackers and the assistant curator of the park, Kimuni Ki Kutota, with a French couple and a Swede on vacation. Since 1970, nearly 30,000 visitors have hiked into the volcanic mountains an hour outside Bukavu to see the gorillas. A few of the shy, reclusive creatures have grown to tolerate them.

"You will see only the ones that allow themselves to be seen—two or three groups in this corner of the park," said Mr. Kimuni. "We believe there are about 250 gorillas here altogether, but you could hike for months and never see the remainder."

A group usually includes half a dozen adults, with an equal number of infants and juveniles. We wound for hours through foliage on the slopes of Mount Kahuzi and its neighbors, looking for the broad trail left as they press through the underbrush. One tracker hacked out a path for us with a razor-sharp machete; two others fanned out on either side, keeping in touch with the leader by emitting low, birdlike whistles.

We were soon soaked from crossing hip-deep streams, from pushing through dew-covered vegetation, and from perspiring in the still, dank air. The environment was not unpleasant, however. There were few insects at the higher elevations, and few brambles. I recall no sense of menace in the forest, only an appreciation for the heavy-scented thickets shaded by a high canopy of 100-foot trees. Yet some caution was necessary. Lone elephants are short-tempered when surprised at close range.

We found a gorilla trail, and conversation fell to a whisper. The tracker in front of me picked up a stem of broken bamboo, noting that the pith had been freshly chewed.

Suddenly from a thicket in front of us came staccato warning sounds, and the lead trackers burst out of the brush in hasty retreat. There are still gorillas here that resent intrusions. We made a wide detour around this irritable fellow, and minutes later sighted a more tolerant neighbor.

It was a dark blotch at first, a moving shadow in the lower limbs of a tree. We approached slowly, until I could see a human-like form stretched languorously along a branch. A hairy arm reached out, a dark hand grasped a *Galium* vine and pulled it toward the mouth with the insouciance of a Roman patrician eating grapes. Then we were too close, and the gorilla slipped quickly down the trunk and disappeared in a crash of underbrush.

Several dozen yards away a young female of nearly 200 pounds appeared suddenly, climbing a straight tree like a telephone lineman, hands wrapped around the back of the trunk while her feet were braced against the front or sides. Perhaps 60 feet up she settled into a comfortable crotch and with powerful arms pulled choice leaves toward her until branches broke with a sharp crack.

The trackers were pointing at something under the overhanging branches of a large tree near us. I bent to see, and at first could make out only a dark mass. Then the massive head of a full-grown female turned slowly toward me and for an instant we locked eyes. I may have imagined the expression on the broad face before it turned away, but I had a sudden rush of guilt, a sense that I was intruding upon an intelligence that might value its privacy as much as I do my own.

I longed to see the dominant male, or silverback, so called because of the hair that whitens with maturity. The trackers discouraged me, saying that *le grand mâle,* "the big male," was unpredictable. My look at a mature male had to wait for a return visit to the park, but it was as close as a stranger can get to a gorilla in the wild, short of shaking his hand. He was resting flat on his back, arms flung behind his head, when we filed quietly into a small leafy clearing. He looked at us, then turned away, rolling onto his side and throwing a thick forearm across his eyes.

In hushed tones we marveled at the powerful neck and shoulders, tapering down to the cowboy-trim hips and bowed legs. He was a healthy male perhaps 25 years old, weighing 300 pounds or more. Jim set up a tripod barely a dozen feet from the dozing beast and began photographing.

With a sigh of resignation the gorilla raised himself to all fours and contemplated us. Rearing suddenly, he hooted several times; he cupped his palms and beat a rapid tattoo on his chest—*pok-pok-pok-pok-pok.*

It was more a request for privacy than a threat. He moved off several feet, sat down, and gazed in another direction. We had plenty of room to leave, and his seeming assurance that he would not even notice if we chose to do so. We obliged him.

For the next stage of our journey to the Ruwenzori, we joined local travelers in a five-hour boat ride to Goma, at the north end of Lake Kivu. We sat at the open fantail, admiring the green hills and savoring fresh pineapple bought during brief mail stops at lakeside villages.

Just outside Goma, a lakeside town with a hint of frontier atmosphere, rises Nyiragongo, one of a string of still-active volcanoes. A nearly perfect cone, its outer shell slants steeply upward to form a chalice roughly 4,125 feet across. That cup holds molten rock.

At 10 o'clock on January 10, 1977, the cone sprang a leak—at least five fissures. A fiery river rushed toward Goma, obliterating crops and engulfing hapless villagers. As many as a hundred people may lie entombed in hardened lava several meters thick. We saw that rock, curled and cracked into jagged edges, as we drove north by rented van.

Our driver for two weeks was a tall Tutsi named Pierre Indoha, a member of the deposed royal family of Rwanda. He drew stares from the Nande people of northern Kivu, not just because of his six-foot-six-inch frame— memory of the warrior past of the Watutsi has not yet faded in Zaire.

On the main highway our speed seldom rose above 20 kilometers, or 12.4 miles, an hour. It fell to a crawl as we eased through crater-like chuckholes or tip-tired along the ridges of deep ruts, cut by trucks. Vehicles were far outnumbered by pedestrians: an almost constant stream of school-bound youngsters, farmers carrying vegetables to market, women bent under heavy loads of firewood. Polygyny is lawful, and common, here. Pierre, who has only one wife, commented with a smile, "We have a joke: that two able wives are as good as one tractor."

Pedestrian traffic diminished as the forested hills leveled out and we entered Virunga National Park, a game refuge of broad, open expanses.

An escarpment called the Mitumba Mountains loomed darkly, west of the plain. Beneath it a windswept sea of grass rippled in the sun, broken only by a few trees and acacia bushes. A line of greenery marked the Rutshuru River. Finally we glimpsed the white-washed structures of Rwindi Lodge, a welcome sight after our washing-machine ride. It was our home for three days, in an animal-watcher's paradise.

Gold in the sunlight, bristle-like feathers make the crowned crane one of Africa's loveliest birds. Male and female bear the same adornment. They breed in swampy areas, which along Lake Kivu's 55-mile length still support sizable populations.

Sunday morning was bright, but still cool, when our van slowed on one of the narrow park roads to squeeze past a truck, whose church-bound human cargo sang in Swahili about a paradise not of this earth. The refrain *"Asifiwe—Let Him be praised"* washed through our open windows in sonorous harmony, then diminished behind us. We prodigals headed for a morning of fishing in the Rutshuru.

This was fishing as I first knew it on the south fork of Iowa's English River—with worms for bait, a bobber, line tied to a rigid pole. And with a few differences. We sought not bullheads but a scaly fish called tilapia. Hippos, gray rocks at mid-river, oinked at us. An armed guard paced the bank nearby, alert for lions. I yanked a dozen tilapia onto the bank before yielding to the noonday heat and returning to the lodge. Early morning and evening were reserved for cruising park roads while standing upright in the van, upper bodies thrust through the open sunroof, alert for game.

Easiest to spot were kob, the trim, light-brown antelope with ridged horns that curve like a shallow question mark. Among them were a few of the larger topi, walnut-colored with bluish blobs on their quarters as if they had lain in puddles of ink. Waterbuck seemed warier.

The largest tusks I have seen in the wild protruded from the jaws of Virunga's elephants, survivors in the war against ivory poachers. Among Africa's animals, there is no sight more majestic than these mountainous gray bodies moving across the plain with a fluid grace, ears waving like huge fans, trunks raised to catch the scent of visitors.

We would have missed many animals had it not been for the eagle eyes of Pierre. "Let's concentrate on finding lions this time," I suggested one afternoon. *"Simba!"* he hissed suddenly, pointing to a lone bush on the plain. In its scant shade panted two young full-maned lions, with a lioness lying spraddle-legged nearby. Pierre parked within 50 feet of them. I cranked the roof to a lion-proof slit and stuck my head through for an unobstructed look.

The nearest male bared his long canines. I raised myself a little higher, and received a second warning; in one lightning-fast move he gathered his feet beneath him and froze my blood with a thunderous cough that seemed to emerge from the bottom of an oil drum.

The lioness stood up, yawned, batted at one of the males as lightly as a house cat, then strolled off through the grass. We followed, slowly, as she moved from clump to clump of grass over a quarter-mile radius, sparring playfully with a lion at each spot. I counted seven more. We hoped to see a hunt, but the pride dawdled until dark.

Even without the spectacle of a kill, a visit to Virunga Park is a review of earth's savage and simplistic origins. As we cruised this broad plain on late afternoons, the sun dropping behind the darkening Mitumba Range and sending out long shadows, a mood of timelessness prevailed. In an increasingly complicated world a sense of earth's beginnings, of the awesome truths of life and death, can provide a renewing wisdom.

But farms and villages press in from all sides. How long before the virgin plains are scorched and plowed? Then Virunga's daily drama will stop while cattle replace the antelope and buffalo and lions are shot as pests. The world will not be poorer when such refuges disappear. It will be bankrupt. . . .

Up numerous switchbacks we climbed the Mitumba Range by car, bound north. Then we would cross a branch of the Great Rift to the east bank, the Ruwenzori. Our road forked as we left a town called Lubero. "The left fork is shorter," said Pierre, "but the right has better scenery. The people here call it 'beauty road.' " We opted for beauty, and found a valley as lush and well-patterned as an intricate quilt. Small-scale African agriculture is often a hodgepodge of slash-and-burn plots. In this valley the rolling hills bore symmetrical plantings of corn, coffee trees, bananas, and sweet potatoes, interrupted occasionally by soft-textured pools of wheat.

Kambala Mutumwa, a local schoolteacher, assured us that the residents of this region, Masareka, were as delighted with it as we were. "Yes, yes," he said, "it is a very beautiful place! The people here are very proud of it, and they are very healthy. The climate is good, and they eat well."

Moreover, they seemed industrious and clever. Two women walked by with heavy loads of firewood, the first dragging a small branch. I suddenly realized that the second was blind, and was following the scraping sound on the dry ground.

Youngsters showed ingenuity too. At one incline several were taking turns coasting on a homemade wooden scooter, a well-engineered vehicle with hand-carved front forks and a swiveling steering post. It supported 175 pounds when I tried it, followed by a shrieking crowd.

How long did it take to build this fine machine, I asked its creator, a modest 13-year-old named Kakulle.

"Two days," he answered shyly, "but most of that time was spent finding the right wood."

Other homemade playthings seen at roadside included little skeletal trucks made from bent wire soldered together, with front wheels cantilevered for steering.

Kivu Province's most prominent business couple began by driving the big trucks the youngsters try to copy.

"We began with one," 38-year-old Victor Ngezayo told me at the family home at Beni. "I would drive day and night, and Brigitte would find out what was needed around the country so that we always carried goods in demand."

"He had his limits, and it was time to leave," says the author of this gorilla in Kahuzi-Biega National Park. The ape endured the visitors' gaze awhile, then moved off, as if to snub them.

The truck became a fleet, and now the Ngezayo ventures include agriculture, coffee export, an air charter service with nine planes, an interest in a chain of hotels.

"Anybody working hard with initiative and imagination can make a fortune here," said Victor, whose muscular shoulders still bear witness to wrestling trucks over Zairian roads. "This country is wide open for development of services, agriculture, you name it. The government will practically give land to people as long as they make improvements."

"Victor handles the export-import business and I deal with local commerce," said Brigitte as she drove us to farmland they have wrested from a tangle of forest. "I also manage our farming operations," she explained, her face lighting up with excitement. Their Brown Swiss cattle graze hock-deep in Kikuyu grass, introduced from Kenya, behind barbed wire strung from crooked posts—a scene that suggested the old American West.

"We cleared about 1,000 hectares [2,500 acres] in five years," said

Brigitte. "We sometimes had 400 people working at it, with axes, hoes, and machetes. Now we're providing fresh milk, cheese, and butter to a community that had none before."

The Ngezayos fly their own plane to keep track of business nationwide.

"I wish we had just one good main road connecting us with the rest of the world so we could move things around easily," said Victor. "No more than that. Too many roads will change the way of life. People here are happy. They rise early, do some work, maybe go hunting or fishing. I would hate to see them start rushing around, meeting schedules, making trinkets for tourists."

The words "just one good road" haunted me as we crossed the Rift Valley on the last leg of our journey—the 40-kilometer drive to the village of Mutwanga. Untimely dry-season rain had left puddles in the ruts, and heavy trucks had gouged them even deeper. At one point, despite Pierre's skill, the tires slipped and we were high-centered, the weight of the van on its axles, the wheels spinning without purchase. After long minutes a large truck approached, with husky young men as passengers. They leaped out and by sheer weight of numbers pushed our vehicle off its perch.

The day was hazy and overcast, the skyline and the forested valley floor a bland whiteout. Near Mutwanga a dark mass like a storm front appeared ahead. Then, like giant monoliths the Ruwenzori towered thousands of feet before us. They looked very steep and very, very high.

"It is a wonderful climb!" Our host for the night, a gregarious Belgian planter named Jacques Ingels, sat with us on his veranda, admiring the mountains in the swiftly fading light. "I am 52 years old and want to climb it one more time." He seemed to have energy enough for many more ascents.

As we drove toward our starting point we saw part of Zaire's energy caught in idle frustration. We were passing a two-room mud-and-stick schoolhouse when a group of children scurried inside. Curious, we stopped and found second- and third-year students sitting primly on their wooden benches, staring straight ahead at the empty teacher's chair.

"Où est le professeur?" asked Jacques, and in each room the answer was the same: The teacher had not come that day.

"It happens often," Jacques told me. "But you can't blame the teachers completely. Often they are not paid because someone above them keeps the money. So they often fail to show up for work."

"Who is the best student?" I asked the lower class, and a boy in back raised his hand. No one disputed his claim. "Why don't you teach the class?" I suggested. His eyes widened in surprise. Hesitantly he walked to the chalkboard and began writing the day's lesson.

Jacques's bookkeeper, a young Zairian named Jean-Pierre, had once been a teacher. He drilled the third-year class on multiplication tables. "Trois fois six?—Three times six?" A dozen arms waved frantically. Jean-Pierre pointed to a petite girl in a ragged dress. Standing, arms stiffly at her side, she said primly, "Trois fois six font dix-huit—eighteen."

I peeked through a hole in the mud wall to see how my young professor was doing. His face stern, he was chopping the air with a rigid hand, warning two restless charges to sit down: "Asseyez-vous, asseyez-vous!"

At an open-air market in Mutwanga we bought fresh beef, manioc, eggs, pineapple, rice, and freshly baked bread—provisions for ourselves and porters. We hired six lean-limbed Banande men in their late teens and a guide named Paul, slightly older and distinctly dignified. He wore shoes, but the others were barefoot. "It's cold at the top," we protested; "there will be snow." Paul shrugged: "They have been there before."

Just before noon we set off with a chattering entourage of the curious. They turned back as the trail began to rise through groves of banana plants and fields of coffee trees. Nearly two hours out we passed the last cassava patch and were swallowed by thick rain forest, but the trail was clear.

As at Kahuzi-Biega, the undergrowth was luxuriant with ferns, creepers, and a few giant fronds of wild banana, all beneath a taller umbrella of trees. The canopy was broken enough to allow glimpses of the mountains ahead. The grandest—Speke, Baker, Stanley—were wreathed in clouds. Once a troop of small monkeys chattered at us. Except for a few birds and the welcome gurgle of swift streams, however, the forest was silent. Animals wary of man, the hunter, do not advertise their presence to man, the hiker.

This, our first day of climbing, may have been the most grueling: Jim and I did not yet have our mountain legs. If memory were perfect we might never climb mountains but once. I recall that five-hour trek as a romantic one, with a vague recollection of getting tired. Then I check my field notes, jerky hieroglyphics written by a hand trembling from exertion. "Another hour is behind us," this weary stranger wrote, adding in despair, "Paul says we may be halfway to the next hut."

Energy and enthusiasm spark a third-grade arithmetic class in a two-room mud-and-stick school at Mutwanga. Teachers, disillusioned by no or low pay, often play hooky, as they did the day the author paid a visit. Another adult visitor led the multiplication drills. In the second grade, star pupil Paluku Kiringwa took over as professor (opposite) for a lesson conducted in French—still Zaire's official language, and used in the public schools throughout the nation.

Finally, at a tumbling rock-strewn stream I was refreshed by two things: the splashing of icy water on my face, neck, and arms, and Paul's announcement that the first hut was less than 15 minutes away. Rwindi Lodge—or the Ritz—was never a more welcome sight than this clapboard structure with uneven floors, reed mattresses, and a population of mouselike voles. On one of the walls a visitor had written: *"Les merveilles de sommet effacent la fatigue. Courage.*—The marvels of the summit are worth the fatigue. Have courage!"

By noon on the second day we were above the rain forest. The creepers crept away, replaced by mountain heather and the first of that spongelike textured moss. The straight, towering deciduous trees gave way to low conifers, twisted like gnomes tortured by the thinning air. We were tested as well. To the ache in our legs was added the rasp of straining breath.

Yet our minds may be the heaviest burden. I climb more easily when I do not worry about slowing down faster climbers or taxing slower ones.

"Paul," I said at a rest stop, "I'm going on early and let the rest of you catch up. I like to climb alone." *"C'est vrai?*—Really?" Highly sociable, as most Zairians seem to be, he was surprised, but assured me that the route was unmistakable. It was. I reached the second hut alone before 1:30, and sat down to enjoy long pulls on my canteen and the glorious sight of the white glaciers of the Ruwenzori, still a day's hike away.

We began that hike through the so-called "root section." It should be called the Enchanted Wood or Middle Earth, for this was a fairyland surely visited at some time by the brothers Grimm or by Tolkien.

Green, yellow, and sometimes reddish moss covered everything to a depth of several feet. Like a lumpy carpet it rounded off the terrain, hiding a boulder here, a fallen branch there, the sharp edge of an upturned rock. It looked soft, and was. Sprawling on my back for a rest at trailside, I continued to sink for several bemused seconds—and close examination revealed a network of tiny living stars.

Carpet beneath, lace above. The conifer branches trailed strands of a wispy, dollar-green lichen. Passage of many feet along the path had worn away the moss, baring the roots beneath. Twisted, curved, knobby, and always slick, they formed an interlocking maze that had to be stepped on, stepped over, and in the steepest parts, climbed like a ladder.

Here and there large holes gaped below overhanging rocks or fallen tree trunks—hobbit homes or gremlin caves, depending on your frame of mind. Mine was benign. At a deliberate pace meant to preserve both energy and balance on ankle-wrenching roots, I advanced as in a dream through one of the most enchanting walks of my life, in an absolute vacuum of silence.

Suddenly I came upon an open slope dotted with the first of the eerie giant lobelia and groundsel. Now the low oxygen of 12,000 feet was extremely noticeable. I shuffled along in slow motion, each step the length of each shoe, inhaling at one step, exhaling with the other.

At the top of that slope, bushes of heather—shoulder-high on the moors of Scotland—stretched far above my head. I followed the ridge several hundred yards, panted up one more steep slope, and stood before the third and final hut, at 14,119 feet.

Fog teased us with glimpses of the next day's goals—a rocky promontory called Wasuwameso and behind it the white cap of the glaciers. For a few moments, Mounts Stanley, Speke, and Baker sparkled against blue sky. Then a gray mist rolled in to envelop us in chilly murk.

Mountaintop triumph was tempered by a mountain malady: altitude sickness, an oxygen deficiency. Headaches and queasy stomachs afflicted all of us. We suggested to Paul that we reach our goals in time to spend the next evening down at the second hut. He translated this into Nande for the porters. Was it altitude sickness or superstition that made their faces break with relief? The Banande long believed that occupying the Ruwenzori were spirits capable of harming trespassers by rolling rocks at them.

My own sleep was troubled that night, but not by spirits or hyrax screams. I was awakened by hyperventilation as my lungs sought more oxygen, even in repose. First light was welcome—and as usual, clear of mist.

It took only half an hour to reach the summit of Wasuwameso, which in Nande means "where the eye never grows tired of looking." Aptly named. From 14,850 feet, the highest point in our climb, a cavalcade of peaks and hills lay before us. Fatigue was forgotten. Below, and perhaps 1,000 feet apart, were natural reservoirs for glacial runoff, named for their colors, Green Lake and Black Lake. Far, far below and dim in the dry-season haze I could make out toylike structures in Mutwanga, with the Rift Valley stretching beyond.

From the hut to the glacier Paul and one porter went with us. At the edge of Green Lake Jim tarried to photograph while I pushed on.

I started up the last slope in my shuffling gait, the thin air seeming to suck energy from me. The porter fell behind, brow furrowed by headache. I reached the top and saw the lower end of the glacier, curled like an eagle's talon gripping the mountainside.

Caching my pack, I began climbing over the moraine, a jumble of rock bulldozed ahead of the ice. Halfway to the snowy mass I turned aside. The act of touching snow virtually at the Equator suddenly became unimportant. I was looking for something else.

The road to the Ruwenzori had been a marvel of new sights and sounds, but one shared with many before me. The register we signed at Mutwanga had shown 75 names, those who hiked this trail in the previous six months. The range is a remote and little-used fragment of the world, but not unknown. I longed for some small nook where, just maybe, no one had trod.

Dwarfed by Nyiragongo Volcano's rim, climbers rest on the edge of the cloud-filled crater (right). Their hike up the 11,380-foot peak, one of eight Virunga volcanoes, took more than four hours. Nyiragongo erupted without warning in 1977 and killed scores of people; the caldera—more than three-quarters of a mile wide—now cups molten as well as solidified lava (below). At night the heat becomes visible in a glow of sullen red.

I scaled a lichen-covered boulder several stories high and walked along its crest. I rock-hopped across a nondescript pool and prepared to try a talus slope. I looked to my right and saw a ten-foot heap of rocks piled against a sheer wall. Against it, or just near it? I climbed the pile to look at the other side, if there was another side.

There was: a recess a dozen yards wide, containing a quiet pool of glacial seep. I scrambled down to sit beside the pool, feeling that on a crowded planet I had found

one perfectly pristine place, a secret corner in the attic of the world that may be known only to me. Its very purity seemed to call for a cleansing. Stripping, I stood ankle-deep and bathed in its skin-tingling chill.

Now, back in a world of asphalt, traffic, chemical smells, and noise, I carry with me the memory of that unspoiled niche. If I never see it again, it is important to know that it exists.

If you find it, by these descriptions, please grant me two favors: Don't mark it to show that you were there, and don't let me know that you were. Consider it your own, and I'll do the same.

Women and children gather to check the catch as fishermen come home to Vitshumbi, a village of 3,000 inhabitants on Lake Idi Amin Dada. Each evening the men row out on the 800-square-mile expanse; they seine all night, then return late in the morning to divide the fish—40 percent to themselves and 60 to the community cooperative established in 1949. Cork floats from the nets fill a section in the lead boat. Below, a platoon of white pelicans converges on the returning fleet to cadge fish heads and other scraps— a daily routine. In one day a five-foot-long white pelican consumes about four pounds of fish. Tilapia, most common haul of Vitshumbi fishermen and the economic mainstay of the village, grill slowly over a bed of glowing, smoky charcoal (right).

FOLLOWING PAGES: *Stalking the dusty street of Vitshumbi, marabou storks scavenge for edible refuse. More watch from their rooftop perches. The men's daily catch, once 20 tons, now averages only 8. The co-op's manager, Kungerwa Bahingo Mupanda, says: "If we could get all the materials we need—nets and motors, replacement parts for the boats—we could feed all Zaire."*

At the end of the rainbow, fields of banana, coffee, and cassava scale the hills of Kivu Province. The area's volcanic soils, among the richest in Zaire, also produce most of the nation's tea and sugar, but the farming methods limit production and unreliable transportation hampers distribution. Highways—narrow, and unpaved—prove undependable. Heavy rains often wash out the only link between two cities; ruts and potholes snag passing vehicles. Deep in the Ituri Forest of Upper Zaire Province, home of the country's earliest inhabitants—the Pygmies—a truck with a broken axle blocked traffic for 40 minutes (below) until volunteers shoved it to the side of the road. Noel Grove and Jim Sugar did not escape such frustrations. On their way to the Ruwenzori, their van stuck fast in a huge rut. They sat for an hour until a truckload of burly young men happened along and dislodged it (bottom).

JAN ZAHLER (ABOVE)

Nostrils flaring, heads high, Cape buffalo confront intruders in Virunga National Park. Mud from a nearby wallow coats their massive horns and tough hides. Many hunters consider this beast the most dangerous big-game animal in Africa; a bull weighs nearly a ton and charges at speeds up to 35 mph. Its heavily bossed skull makes a head shot nearly impossible.

Fading sunlight bathes a pride of lions—a male and two females—on a short-grass plain at Virunga. Established by the Belgians in 1925 as Parc National Albert, Virunga ranks as the oldest park of Zaire's seven; it now stretches more than 190 miles from Lake Kivu to the Ruwenzori. Great herds roam the savannas near Lake Idi Amin: among them, Uganda kob (below) and elephants. More elephants survive in Zaire than anywhere else in Africa.

Bellowing at a rival in a Virunga mudhole, a bull hippopotamus bares the enormous chisel-like lower teeth that serve as his major weapon. The rivers and wallows of Virunga National Park shelter the world's largest concentration of hippos. They emerge from the water to graze at night, when each three-ton animal consumes as much as forty pounds of grass.

FOLLOWING PAGES:
Clipped and clean, cottages south of Beni reflect the care and pride of their inhabitants, who call this thoroughfare "beauty road." Houses hug the highways throughout Zaire, so many a village blurs into the next.

"Anybody working hard with initiative and imagination can make a fortune here,"
insists 38-year-old entrepreneur Victor Ngezayo with his wife, Brigitte, in their Beni coffee
warehouse. Victor started as a truck driver at age 19; now he and Brigitte own a fleet of
trucks, a coffee export business, an air charter service, and an interest in a chain of hotels.
They provide advice and credit to employees undertaking business ventures of their own.
At the depot of the Ngezayos' coffee company, Capaco, women sort beans into three grades
according to color. Lightest beans rank highest. Nursing mothers bring their children to work;
the family can share the labor, and the time spent together strengthens the bonds of kinship
that claim allegiance in African societies.

*Mammoth fronds of an eight-foot-high wild banana crowd ferns and creepers in
a thicket along the lower Ruwenzori trail (above, left). As the path winds upward,
spongy sphagnum moss (above, top) carpets twisted roots and slippery boulders,
making the trek difficult and dangerous. At higher elevations, alchemilla,
a perennial herb (above), forms dense meadows. In a forbidding wood (opposite)
wisps of a lichen called old man's beard dangle from giant heathers, and the white
blooms of everlastings rise above a cluttered forest floor. Here, near the summit, two
of the Ruwenzori's strangest plants first appear; a huge spike of tree lobelia
in the left background looms above the cabbagelike leaves of a groundsel at center.*

Gnarled roots, blanketed with thick moss—the author's "Enchanted Wood or Middle Earth"—stretch before him on the second day of the hike (below). Through a maze of trunks and limbs he fought his way up to 12,000 feet, where the Ruwenzori's fantastic plants begin. Like heroes in a fairy tale, he and his party struggled past lobelias, groundsel, and hanging lichens in a silent world of wet and wild greenery.

FOLLOWING PAGES: *Mist shrouds peaks and glaciers near Wasuwameso, high in the Ruwenzori. Trail-weary, the author and the photographer agreed that these summits evoked a mood unique in their experience—at once uncanny and untroubled. No winds stirred; silence imposed itself; remoteness suffused mystery with peace.*

Contributors

A free-lance specialist in wilderness photography, SAM ABELL counts *The Pacific Crest Trail* and *Still Waters, White Waters* among his numerous assignments for the Society. A graduate of the University of Kentucky, he lives near the Virginia mountains.

Growing up abroad in a Foreign Service family, LESLIE ALLEN spent nine years in South America. After receiving a B.A. with honors from Bryn Mawr, she worked as a free-lance writer before joining the Society's staff in 1978. This book marks her first foreign assignment for Special Publications. She now lives in her birthplace, the District of Columbia.

Born in Detroit, JAMES BILLIPP majored in Spanish literature—and took up mountain climbing—at Colgate University. He has visited the Ica of Colombia four times since he first met them in 1974. He now lives in New York City. A producer for WNYC-TV, he also does editing and camera work; his TV credits include a series on the Margaret Mead Film Festival at the American Museum of Natural History.

A native of Norway, TOR EIGELAND studied in Canada, graduated from the University of Guadalajara in Mexico, and has been a free-lance photojournalist for more than twenty years. His work has appeared in many Special Publications since 1966. Today he makes his home in Spain.

Belgian by birth, free-lance photojournalist VICTOR ENGLEBERT has traveled extensively in Africa, Asia, and Latin America, and has contributed to the Society's publications since 1965. He reported on peoples of Africa for *Nomads of the World* and *Primitive Worlds*. Formerly a resident of New York City, he now lives in Cali, Colombia.

Thirteen years with NATIONAL GEOGRAPHIC have taken senior writer NOEL GROVE to far-flung regions—Iceland, North Yemen, Nigeria, Taiwan, and Venezuela among them. In 1976 he described the Alaska Highway in *Alaska: High Roads to Adventure*. A native of Iowa and a graduate of McPherson College in Kansas, he lives in Virginia.

JANE R. McCAULEY, a native of Wilmington, Delaware, earned her B.A. at Guilford College and took graduate courses at the University of North Carolina in Chapel Hill. She lived for three years in Geneva, Switzerland, before joining the Society's staff in 1970; her chapter on Afghanistan is her first for Special Publications. Expert in needlecraft, she takes special interest in textile and fabric arts.

ROLAND and SABRINA MICHAUD, who met in Morocco, have traveled widely in Central Asia. Their work has appeared in two books of their own, *Caravans to Tartary* and *Afghanistan: Paradise Lost*, as well as in European journals and NATIONAL GEOGRAPHIC. For the Special Publication *Nomads of the World*, they photographed the Qashqā'ī of Iran. They make their home in France with their son, Romain.

Free-lance photographer JAMES A. SUGAR, a native of Baltimore, earned a B.A. with honors from Wesleyan University in Connecticut, an M.A. from the University of Pennsylvania. Since 1969 he has worked full time for the Society. For Special Publications he photographed *Railroads: the Great American Adventure* and *America's Sunset Coast*. Today he makes his home in San Francisco.

Acknowledgments

The Special Publications Division is grateful to the individuals, agencies, and organizations portrayed, named, or quoted in this book, and to those cited here, for their assistance in its preparation. In particular, it thanks embassy, tourist office, and local officials of the respective nations, and naval personnel of Argentina and Chile. It thanks specialists at the Geography and Map Division, and the Hispanic Division, of the Library of Congress, the Smithsonian Institution, the Department of Agriculture, the State Department, and the World Bank. Also, as follows:
THE MARQUESAS: Dr. Kenneth P. Emory, Dr. Marie-Helene Sachet, Dr. Yosihiko H. Sinoto, Dr. William V. Sliter, Dr. Robert C. Suggs, Genevieve L. Weiler.
AFGHANISTAN: Ghulam Ali Ayeen, Dr. David C. Champagne, Dr. Louis Dupree, Nancy Hatch Dupree, Nasrine and Max Gross, Dawood Moosa, the Honorable Robert G. Neumann, Dr. M. Nazif Shahrani, Dr. William Trousdale; the Center for Afghanistan Studies; the Textile Museum.
TIERRA DEL FUEGO: Roberto de Andraca, Norman J. Brouwer, Enrique Campos Menéndez, Dr. Ian W. D. Dalziel, Dr. Tom D. Dillehay, Joseph F. Dorsey, Jr., Dr. Theodore R. Dudley, Dr. William L. Franklin, Dr. E. Kenneth Haviland, Manuel Jaime, Nicolás Luco, Dr. James G. Mead, Jennifer Moseley, Dr. Edmundo Pisano, Dr. Alan M. Stahl, Dr. George E. Watson; the British Museum, the Mariners' Museum (Newport News), the National Maritime Museum (Greenwich, England), the U. S. Coast Guard.
THE SANTA MARTAS: Dr. Carlos Angulo Valdés, Dr. Junius Bird, Dr. Alec S. Bright, Dr. Betty J. Meggers, Dr. G. Reichel-Dolmatoff.
THE ALPUJARRAS: Ida Angustia, Dr. Joaquín Bosque Maurel, Dr. James Casey, Dr. Guillermo Céspedes, Sabina and Martin Gardner, Dr. Antonio Gilman, Dr. Thomas F. Glick, Dr. John R. Hébert, Dr. Dixon Hubbard, Dr. Geoffrey Parker, the Reverend Miguel Peinado Martínez, Dr. Josep M. Sola-Solé, Montserrat Ybero Cobos.
THE RUWENZORI: Adrien de Schreyver, Dr. Robert Faden, Dr. Dian Fossey, Roger Frazier, Jacques Guillot-Lageat, Warren Littrell, Lindsay McClelland, Willett Weeks.

Index

Boldface indicates illustrations; *italic* refers to picture captions

Additional Reading

The reader may wish to consult the *National Geographic Index* for pertinent articles, and to refer to the following:

THE MARQUESAS: Gavan Daws, *A Dream of Islands;* Greg Dening, *Islands and Beaches;* E. S. Craighill Handy, *The Native Culture in the Marquesas;* Robert C. Suggs, *Hidden Worlds of Polynesia.*

AFGHANISTAN: Pierre Centlivres, *Un bazar d'Asie Centrale;* C.-J. Charpentier, *Bazaar-e Tashqurghan;* Nancy Hatch Dupree, *The Road to Balkh;* Angus Hamilton, *Afghanistan;* Hasan Kawun Kakar, *Government and Society in Afghanistan;* Roland and Sabrina Michaud, *Caravans to Tartary;* Nancy and Richard Newell, *The Struggle for Afghanistan.*

TIERRA DEL FUEGO: E. Lucas Bridges, *Uttermost Part of the Earth;* Bruce Chatwin, *In Patagonia;* Charles Darwin, *The Voyage of the Beagle;* Rae Natalie Prosser Goodall, *Tierra del Fuego;* Richard Hough, *The Blind Horn's Hate;* Samuel Eliot Morison, *The European Discovery of America: The Southern Voyages* A.D. *1492-1616;* Eric Shipton, *Tierra del Fuego: The Fatal Lodestone;* Alan Villiers, *The War with Cape Horn.*

THE SANTA MARTAS: Edward J. Goodman, *The Explorers of South America;* J. A. Mason, *Archaeology of Santa Marta, Colombia;* Tony Morrison, *Land Above the Clouds: Wildlife of the Andes;* Brian Moser and Donald Taylor, *The Cocaine Eaters;* Willard S. Park, "Tribes of the Sierra Nevada de Santa Marta, Colombia," in *Handbook of South American Indians,* vol. 2; G. Reichel-Dolmatoff, *Colombia.*

THE ALPUJARRAS: Gerald Brenan, *South From Granada;* Julio Caro Baroja, *Los moriscos del Reino de Granada;* Anwar G. Chejne, *Muslim Spain;* John H. Elliott, *Imperial Spain: 1469-1716;* Thomas F. Glick, *Islamic and Christian Spain in the Early Middle Ages;* Washington Irving, *Chronicle of the Conquest of Granada;* Francisco Izquierdo, *El apócrifo de la Alpujarra Alta;* José A. Tapia Garrido, *Historia de la Alpujarra Baja.*

THE RUWENZORI: Siradiou Diallo, *Zaire Today;* H. A. Osmaston and D. Pasteur, *Guide to the Ruwenzori;* George B. Schaller, *The Mountain Gorilla, Ecology and Behavior;* Henry M. Stanley, *In Darkest Africa;* Patrick M. Synge, *Mountains of the Moon;* Haroun Tazieff, *Nyiragongo, the Hidden Volcano;* Crawford Young, *Politics in the Congo.*

**Library of Congress Cataloging in
Publication Data**
Main entry under title:
Secret corners of the world.
    Bibliography: p.
    Includes index.
    Contents: The Marquesas / by Vic-
tor Englebert—Northern Afghanistan /
by Jane McCauley—Tierra del Fuego / by
Leslie B. Allen—[etc.]
    1. Voyages and travels—1951-
—Addresses, essays, lectures.   I.
National Geographic Society.
Special Publications Division.
G465.S39   910.4   81-48073
                                AACR2
ISBN 0-87044-412-3 (regular binding)
ISBN 0-87044-412-4 (library binding)

Composition for *Secret Corners of the World* by National Geographic's Photographic Services, Carl M. Shrader, Chief, Lawrence F. Ludwig, Assistant Chief. Printed and
bound by Holladay-Tyler Printing Corp., Rockville, Md. Color separations by the
Lanman Progressive Corp., Washington, D. C.; Lincoln Graphics, Inc., Cherry Hill,
N.J.; N.E.C., Inc., Nashville, Tenn.

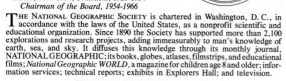